# Praise f(
## Mentoring Conversations

'There are many books about mentoring but few books for mentoring. Tony Horsfall, after 20 years of practice and reflection, now provides such a book. This is not a book about how mentoring should (or shouldn't) be done, but a kind of atlas of potential conversation starters, charting the many personal and theological issues that may arise within a journey of faith. Each chapter is short and snappy, as well as being both biblically rooted and pastorally sensitive. The chapters also provide plenty of opportunities for going deeper into specific issues, with insightful discussion questions and recommended reading. This book will be a handy resource for mentors and mentees as they explore the great issues of Christian discipleship together.'
**Aaron Edwards, lecturer and programme lead for the MA Mission and Christian Mentoring pathway at Cliff College, Derbyshire**

'In this insightful book, Tony Horsfall reminds us that conversation is at the heart of a spiritual mentoring relationship. Tony invites us to reflect upon the conversations we enter into with our mentoring practice, asking us to engage in "holy conversation". Covering topics foundational to Christian spiritual formation with clarity, this book is an essential practical resource to draw upon and a must read for all those who are serving as a mentor today.'
**Jennie Fytche, training provider and mentor, The Christian Coach and Mentor Network**

'This wonderful book will make an excellent tool, enabling both mentor and mentee to walk together with God. It will provoke conversation, reminding them of what God has already done in their lives, and offer practical teaching to increase a sense of his presence and purpose for the future. Rooted in scripture, it will help answer the heart cry of many for a deeper walk with Jesus. I am delighted to commend this volume to anyone who is serious about following Christ.'
**Andy Lancaster, pastoral care leader, Bridge Community Church, Leeds**

'Another gem of a book from Tony. It is written in a conversational style that is easy to read and yet has some deep thoughts on the area of mentoring. I loved the questions at the end of each chapter to help mentor and mentee alike move on in their spiritual journey. This book will be a must for my "holy conversations" in mentoring – I will definitely be using it with all of my mentees.'
**Sharon Prior, senior lecturer, Moorlands College**

'*Mentoring Conversations* will be an invaluable resource for Christian mentors who want to engage their mentees in searching and transformative dialogue. The wide range of topics makes it suitable for use with Christians at any stage of faith who have a desire to grow as disciples of Jesus. Although it is written primarily with a one-to-one mentoring relationship in mind, I can also see this book being useful for those engaged in peer mentoring or even small spiritual formation groups. Each topic has the potential to be a catalyst for transformation and growth. I am excited about adding this to my own mentoring resources.'
**Major Jane Alton, Salvation Army officer, church leader and Christian mentor**

'Tony Horsfall is recognised and respected as an elder statesman in the area of mentoring, and this book is a gift to those of us who have been inspired and encouraged by him. In its down-to-earth and biblically based focus on the growth of the individual, it mirrors Tony's own approach to any conversation you have with him – you leave feeling encouraged, challenged and that you have had his undivided attention! I shall use this mentoring tool, which is riddled with insights and wisdom, widely in my own mentoring, both formally and informally.'
**Paul Wilcox, The Christian Coach and Mentor Network, author of *Intentional Mentoring***

'Another rich yet practical book from Tony Horsfall. As more churches and missions become aware of the value of mentoring relationships, this book is a timely gift with the comprehensive range of topics included. The conversation starters will assist experienced mentors to take interactions to a deeper level and will be a godsend to people new to mentoring.'
**Christine Perkins, Pioneers UK member care for single women**

# Mentoring Conversations

## 30 key topics to explore together

## Tony Horsfall

BRF

**The Bible Reading Fellowship**
15 The Chambers, Vineyard
Abingdon OX14 3FE
**brf.org.uk**

The Bible Reading Fellowship (BRF) is a Registered Charity (233280)

ISBN 978 0 85746 925 0
First published 2020
10 9 8 7 6 5 4 3 2 1 0
All rights reserved

**Acknowledgements**
Unless otherwise stated, scripture quotations are taken from The Holy Bible, New International Version (Anglicised edition) copyright © 1979, 1984, 2011 by Biblica. Used by permission of Hodder & Stoughton Publishers, a Hachette UK company. All rights reserved. 'NIV' is a registered trademark of Biblica. UK trademark number 1448790.

Scripture quotations marked MSG are taken from *The Message*, copyright © 1993, 1994, 1995, 1996, 2000, 2001, 2002 by Eugene H. Peterson. Used by permission of NavPress. All rights reserved. Represented by Tyndale House Publishers, Inc.

Scripture quotations marked RSV are taken from The Revised Standard Version of the Bible, copyright © 1946, 1952, 1971 by the Division of Christian Education of the National Council of the Churches of Christ in the United States of America. Used by permission. All rights reserved.

Every effort has been made to trace and contact copyright owners for material used in this resource. We apologise for any inadvertent omissions or errors, and would ask those concerned to contact us so that full acknowledgement can be made in the future.

A catalogue record for this book is available from the British Library

Printed and bound by TJ Books Limited

*To the memory of my dear wife, Evelyn (1947–2020),*
*who sacrificially gave herself to support me in my ministry,*
*especially that of writing.*
*Nothing I have achieved would have been possible without her.*

# Contents

## GOING DEEPER

## STAYING STRONG

## LIVING WITH MYSTERY

# Introduction

I first became involved in mentoring some 20 years ago when mentoring was still a fairly new concept in most churches. Since then the effectiveness of working one-to-one with others for their spiritual growth has become accepted as part of the ministry philosophy of many churches and organisations. Now a variety of training courses exist to equip people for a ministry of mentoring, many offering recognised qualifications.

All this is very exciting, but it has left me wondering how those who have been trained as mentors are progressing in their ministry. Are they finding it easy or difficult? Specifically, I wonder what resources they have to help them in their calling to make disciples.

I am also concerned for the many people who mentor others informally, without any specific training. They probably never use the term 'mentoring' themselves, but that is what they do as they quietly draw alongside others to help them in following Jesus. What resources do they have, I wonder?

I suspect that those mentors who are already experienced in life and ministry will have a good idea of what the Christian journey looks like and what are the key areas to cover in their times of conversation with those they are helping. Others, however, may not be so confident or well equipped. Their ministry of mentoring may never really get off the ground because they are less sure of which topics are important in a mentoring relationship. To meet this need I have written *Mentoring Conversations*, with the purpose of providing material around which a series of mentoring sessions might be based. For those meeting one to one or in a small group, here are 30 key topics to be explored in a mentoring setting that will help in producing mature disciples.

Conversation is at the heart of mentoring. Essentially it is about two or more people meeting together to talk about the journey of faith, usually with the more experienced person taking the lead (the mentor) and the other person or people keen to learn by sharing their questions and concerns (the mentoree). A mentor needs to be a good listener, skilled at asking the kind of questions that lead to deeper sharing and able to make sense of what they are hearing. David Benner, in his book *Sacred Companions*, names the three key ingredients in mentoring as hospitality, presence and dialogue.[1]

*Hospitality* in this sense is welcoming others into our life with the offer of grace and love. It is making time for them and providing a safe space where they can feel accepted and where they are able to share freely their innermost longings and questions without fear of judgement or ridicule.

*Presence* means that we give them our full attention, being present to the other for the time we are together. We place our own concerns to one side so that we can listen well to what is shared. It also reminds us that our aim is to become more aware of God's presence as we meet together.

*Dialogue* is about heartfelt conversation and, as Benner says, 'Dialogue is one of the deepest forms of soul engagement we can experience with another person. It is a gift of inestimable value.'[2] Such conversations involve exploring thoughts and feelings and seeking God's insight for the way ahead. They do not have to be intense, but they are purposeful and hopefully lead to a sharing of one's innermost self.

This is the kind of conversation I have in mind, not merely chit-chat or even Bible study. I am talking about *holy* conversation, the sort of dialogue that includes vulnerable sharing and that leads to a deeper relationship with God and a transformation of life. This is surely at the heart of all discipleship and is the kind of interaction that is described in the book of Malachi: 'Then those who feared the Lord talked with each other, and the Lord listened and heard' (3:16).

Only after I had begun thinking along these lines did I come across the Puritan practice of 'conference'.[3] To confer is to talk with others about things that really matter, and for the Puritans this meant reflective conversation about God and the state of one's soul. Joanne Jung, in her book *The Lost Discipline of Conversation*, seeks to restore this forgotten practice to the church today. She writes, 'We can, in conversation, be as Christ to one another, or to another. God desires that our conversations reflect and ultimately direct us and others to Him.'[4]

At a time when there is so much social isolation and shallowness in relationships, such meaningful conversation is vital for our health and well-being and our spiritual vitality. Jung goes on to say, 'For optimal spiritual health, conversations on spiritual matters matter. They speak to our desire to know and be known by God and one another, and to do so in community.'[5]

For the English Puritans of the 16th and 17th centuries, 'conference' was a vitally important means of grace intended to promote spiritual transformation into the likeness of Christ, and it was as familiar to them as prayer or Bible meditation. They revered the Bible and gave high value to preaching, encouraging their followers to pay careful attention to what they heard by listening well, taking notes, repeating the sermon and conferring with others. In this way the word of God could take root in their hearts, resulting in a change of life. The practice of conference was the key to transformation, for it was in the context of honest sharing that the connection was made between biblical truth and life experience. Such conversations could take place over meals or when walking together, in formal ways or more spontaneously, but always the aim was the care of souls and the promotion of spiritual growth.

Perhaps God is reminding us of the importance of good conversation as a key factor in disciple-making and in our own transformation. The 30 topics included in this book have been chosen carefully to encourage such dialogue and provide substance for strategic conversations. As I have reflected on my own journey with God over more than 50 years, I have brought together under six headings some of the issues that have been central to my own spiritual formation. There is a progression to the chapters, but I am not offering here a curriculum for growth that must be slavishly followed. Spiritual growth is far more untidy than that and takes place gradually over a lifetime. Earlier chapters may be more suited to newer believers (although everyone can benefit from revisiting foundational truths), while later ones may be more appropriate for those who are more mature in the faith. You are welcome to choose which chapters to focus on and to leave others that seem less relevant at the moment. Think of *Mentoring Conversations* as a resource book to be dipped into as and when you need it. For this reason, you will find some minor overlapping in the chapters, since it is not expected that you will necessarily read them all.

## How to use this book

I see the book's primary use as being in a one-to-one setting where both mentor and mentoree have a copy of the book. The mentor might suggest reading a particular chapter for discussion before the meeting and then use the questions given as a starting point for conversation. Or it might be the other way round, with the mentoree saying, 'This is the topic that most interests me right now.' Again, having both read the relevant section, the questions can then be used as an aid to deeper dialogue. This is a process that may be repeated with other topics that are deemed relevant.

Equally, the book could be used by a small group (small enough so that deep conversation can happen), where a leader might facilitate the discussion using topics considered most relevant to the group. Each person will need their own copy of the book so they can prepare well beforehand and then come to the group session ready to share their thoughts and ask their questions.

It would also work well for a peer-mentoring group, perhaps comprised of colleagues or friends meeting every so often for a study morning, quiet day or retreat together. Each time they meet, a different person could choose the topic for reflection, discussion and prayer.

The normal pattern for using this material will be in conversation with other people. We do not grow spiritually in isolation, but in company with others. However, because of circumstances some may prefer to work through the book by themselves. This could apply, for example, to those in remote situations or working overseas. In such a scenario, you the reader would be the mentoree and I the author would be your mentor-at-a-distance. This is not ideal, but could still be useful.

Creative people are likely to find ways to use the material in ways that I have not thought of. Please do so! What I hope will happen is that the material within these pages will act as a catalyst for good conversation, leading to spiritual growth and transformation and the making of more mature disciples of Jesus. If that happens, I will be well satisfied.

# Foundations

# 1

# The call to follow

**After this, Jesus went out and saw a tax collector by the name of Levi sitting at his tax booth. 'Follow me,' Jesus said to him, and Levi got up, left everything and followed him.**
LUKE 5:27–28

Foundations are an essential part of any building work. To stand the test of time, a building must have sure foundations. The higher the building, the deeper the foundations.

Gordon MacDonald tells the story of the building of the famous Brooklyn Bridge in New York. The chief engineer was frustrated by public opinion that the work of construction was too slow. He reminded them that as much work was being undertaken underwater as above it and that, in fact, more masonry and concrete were used on the hidden foundations than on the part of the bridge that would be above the waterline. MacDonald comments:

> The Brooklyn Bridge remains a major transportation artery in New York City today because more than 135 years ago the chief engineer and his construction team did their most patient and daring work where no-one could see it: on the foundations of the towers below the waterline.[6]

A mentoring relationship is a good place to examine the foundations on which we are building our life in Christ. This is not a backward step, because our spiritual foundations are crucial to our growth in God, and we do well to check them in case they need strengthening. No matter how long we have been believers, it is always prudent to make sure our foundations are firm and sure. As the apostle Paul said to the church at Corinth: 'Examine yourselves to see whether you are in the faith; test yourselves' (2 Corinthians 13:5).

At the heart of the Christian life is the call to discipleship, to be those who follow Jesus wholeheartedly, modelling our lives on his and seeking to do his will as best we can. As he began his public ministry, Jesus carefully gathered around himself a group of men and women who wanted to do just that. His call to them was unequivocal: 'Come, follow me,' he said (Mark 1:17).

From the different gospel accounts we surmise that he met with them several times before they were ready to take such a bold step, but eventually they were decided. Simon, Andrew, James and John left their fishing nets (their livelihood) and followed him. Soon others joined the band of disciples – Philip and Nathanael (Bartholomew), Matthew (Levi), Thomas, James, Simon the Zealot, Thaddaeus and Judas Iscariot. They gave themselves to being with Jesus, to learning from his teaching and example and to sharing in his ministry.

The message of Jesus that they embraced with such enthusiasm was disarmingly simple, yet deeply challenging: 'The time has come... The kingdom of God has come near. Repent and believe the good news!' (Mark 1:15).

To *repent* is to turn away from sin and anything that is wrong in our lives. It involves a complete change of direction, a turning away from that which is unhelpful and a turning towards that which is good and right in God's sight. This is indeed a radical change, and it is not to be passed over lightly. Repentance is often costly and involves sorrow over the sin in our lives. It is an ongoing attitude of heart that we maintain as we consistently choose to leave our sinful ways behind us and instead choose to follow the way of God.

To *believe* is to accept for ourselves the gospel message. Such belief is not simply an intellectual assent to faith statements (like the Apostles' Creed) but a commitment of heart and life to actually live by the truth we have found in Jesus. It is to recognise Jesus as the Son of God and to receive by faith the grace and forgiveness he offers us through his sacrificial death. It is to trust him in all the circumstances of life.

Those who truly repent and sincerely believe bring themselves under the lordship of Christ and enter the realm of his kingdom. They gladly submit their will to his and make their aim in life to please him. Sadly, this foundational principle is often missing in much western Christianity. We have offered a gospel to people that centres on receiving salvation and forgiveness without any mention of the cost of being a disciple. At best this comes later, for the few who want to take it further, and the call to discipleship is often seen as an optional extra for the spiritual elite. Bill Hull calls this 'non-discipleship

Christianity', seeing it as the major weakness of the contemporary church. He writes, 'We evangelicals accept and encourage a two-level Christian experience in which only serious Christians pursue and practise discipleship, while grace and forgiveness is enough for everyone else.'[7]

When Priscilla and Aquila met Apollos in Ephesus (Acts 18:24–28), they recognised him as a young man who was gifted and zealous for God, yet who needed help in understanding and expressing his faith more fully. With their heart for making disciples, they 'invited him to their home and explained to him the way of God more accurately' (v. 26). Here is a wonderful picture of the kind of mentoring relationship we have in mind, and it is the kind of relationship most believers need if they are to have good foundations and grow to maturity.

If we are to build a life in God that is strong enough to withstand the storms of life and vibrant enough to have a positive impact on others, it will be because this solid foundation of discipleship has been laid in our hearts. Only when we take discipleship seriously for ourselves will we have the authority to make other disciples.

I took my first steps as a disciple of Christ as a 14-year-old, when I responded to an invitation to receive God's free gift of salvation during a service in the tiny Methodist chapel in the village where I grew up. Almost immediately I had a sense that God had a purpose for my life, but I floundered at first as a believer because there was no one to show me the way. Fortunately a new teacher with a strong faith came to the school I attended and began to disciple a small group of us who were believers (he may not have used that term in those days). Through his careful nurturing – and that of my youth group leader – I grew stronger in my faith until I began to sense the call to train for ministry, whatever that might involve.

I am so grateful that those who mentored me back then made clear the claims of Christ: 'Whoever wants to be my disciple must deny themselves and take up their cross and follow me' (Mark 8:34). It was not easy, as there were issues in my life that needed sorting out. But as I increasingly submitted to the claims of Christ, I began to grow stronger in faith and clearer in my life's direction. This good foundation has served me well over the years when other challenges have come my way. I may waver from time to time, but in my heart of hearts I know I am a disciple of Jesus, and my choice is to do his will.

# Conversation starters

1   How would you describe your spiritual foundations? How did you come to faith, and what was your early experience of following Christ?
2   What part has repentance played in your relationship with God? What would you say are the main things you believe?
3   Would you say that 'being a disciple of Jesus' is fundamental to the way you understand yourself? If so, how does it influence the way you live and the choices you make?
4   Can you share an example of costly obedience as you have sought to follow Christ?
5   What challenges do you currently face as you seek to be a disciple of Jesus?

# Helpful reading

Dietrich Bonhoeffer, *The Cost of Discipleship* (Macmillan, 1937)
Bill Hull, *The Complete Book of Discipleship: On being and making followers of Christ* (NavPress, 2006)
Peter Morden, *The Message of Discipleship: Authentic followers of Jesus in today's world* (IVP, 2019)
David Watson, *Discipleship* (Hodder and Stoughton, 1983)
Dallas Willard, *The Great Omission: Reclaiming Jesus's essential teachings on discipleship* (Monarch, 2006)

# 2

# The power of the new birth

**Yet to all who did receive him, to those who believed in his name, he gave the right to become children of God – children born not of natural descent, nor of human decision or a husband's will, but born of God.**

JOHN 1:12–13

Chuck Colson was a leading figure in the White House administration of President Nixon from 1969 to 1973. Known as the 'hatchet man', he was both ruthless and cunning as he sought to weaken the president's enemies. He was involved in the infamous Watergate scandal and was imprisoned for his part in the affair.

When Colson was facing arrest and becoming increasingly conscious of his wrongdoing, a friend gave him a copy of *Mere Christianity* by C.S. Lewis. The book changed his life. He experienced a genuine conversion which sparked a radical change in his life. After his release, he wrote his memoirs in a book entitled *Born Again* and went on to found Prison Fellowship International, a ministry dedicated to supporting prisoners and their families. Colson wrote:

> The real story was that Christ had reached down to me, even in my disgrace and shame, and revealed Himself as the one who forgives and makes new. *Born Again* is the story of a broken man transformed by the love and power of Jesus Christ – who continues to transform me every passing day.[8]

Colson experienced what the Bible calls the new birth, and although his story of conversion is more dramatic than most, all of us who turn in repentance and faith to Christ experience the same transforming spiritual dynamic at work in our hearts. Indeed, such an experience of being born again (or more accurately 'born from above', since the initiative is with God) is a key foundation in the spiritual life.

Jesus made this absolutely clear to Nicodemus, a respected religious leader and spiritual seeker, who came to him secretly one night. 'Very truly I tell you,' Jesus said, 'no one can see the kingdom of God unless they are born again' (John 3:3). He went on to say (v. 5) that we cannot enter the kingdom of God without experiencing both physical birth (born of water) and spiritual birth (born of the Spirit). The experience of new birth is essential if we are to understand and grasp the spiritual dimension to life.

This experience of being born again is also called regeneration, and it is the result of the mysterious work of the Spirit by which the seeds of new life (God's own divine life) are implanted within us. It is a miracle that God works in all those who turn sincerely to him in repentance and faith, and it imparts to us the power to change and to live a new life. Colson did not simply turn over a new leaf; the change in him was not a case of self-reformation. Such a transformation could only be brought about by the direct action of the Spirit of God, and it is the same Spirit who is at work in every believer.

The apostle Paul experienced such a turnaround in his own life. The man who persecuted the church, who described himself as the foremost of sinners, a blasphemer and a violent man, was turned upside down by the grace and mercy of God (1 Timothy 1:12–14). After his encounter with Jesus on the road to Damascus, he became a preacher of the faith, boldly carrying the gospel message throughout the Mediterranean world and being willing to suffer much in the process. He described the startling change that the new birth makes in these inspiring words: 'If anyone is in Christ, the new creation has come: the old has gone, the new is here!' (2 Corinthians 5:17).

Furthermore, he saw it as being like a personal resurrection for those who had once been dead in their trespasses and sins. He said:

> But because of his great love for us, God, who is rich in mercy, made us alive with Christ even when we were dead in transgressions – it is by grace you have been saved.
> EPHESIANS 2:4–5

Those of us for whom conversion was less dramatic and more gradual may underestimate what has actually happened to us, but as we turned to Christ the same seed of divine life was planted in us. Perhaps we need to pause from time to time to remind ourselves of this staggering truth: the life of God is now at work in us, giving us the power to change and to be transformed.

The apostle Peter had also known the transforming work of God in his life, and in his first epistle – most likely written to encourage newly baptised believers – reminds his readers of this same reality: 'You have been born again, not of perishable seed, but of imperishable, through the living and enduring word of God' (1 Peter 1:23). Here is the same picture of the seed of God having been sown into our hearts, hopefully to find fertile ground. Not only does this change us in the initial sense of turning away from our old way of life, but it also makes possible the growth of the new life within us, of Christlikeness and moral transformation.

With this in mind, Peter can exhort his readers to 'grow in the grace and knowledge of our Lord and Saviour Jesus Christ' (2 Peter 3:18). Such an encouragement would be futile were it not for the fact that we are able to change and to grow because of the life that is within us. This transformation never comes about by merely trying harder or living by rules and regulations. It is made possible by nurturing the seed of divine life within us.

My wife is a keen gardener, and she loves plants. In particular she likes to grow things from seed. She can often be found pottering in the greenhouse, sowing her seeds in little plastic trays and plant pots, making sure they have the right conditions in which to grow and thrive. Carefully over the weeks she nurtures and tends them as they begin to sprout and grow, transplanting them when necessary, watering and feeding them as required. Patiently she cooperates with the power of nature, taking great delight in the whole process, until finally she can see the results – beautiful flowers, healthy vege-tables, rosy-red tomatoes.

If a person can take such care over plants, surely we can take care over our souls? As we learn to work in harmony with the new life within us and to live in keeping with the ways of the Spirit of God, we will be changed and transformed from within. As Paul reminds the Galatians, we reap what we sow: 'The one who plants in response to God, letting God's Spirit do the growth work in him, harvests a crop of real, eternal life' (Galatians 6:8, MSG).

## Conversation starters

1  Have you experienced the new birth? How did it come about, and how has it changed your life?
2  Why is the new birth essential to our spiritual growth and development as disciples?
3  What do you learn from the picture of the life of God being like a seed sown in your heart?
4  Why do you think trying harder to live like a Christian is futile? What is a better alternative?
5  How are you nurturing the life of God within you?

## Helpful reading

James M. Boice, *Amazing Grace* (Tyndale House, 1993)
Dan Clark, *I'm a Christian, Aren't I?* (IVP, 2010)
Billy Graham, *How to be Born Again* (Word Publishing, 1977)
David Pawson, *The Normal Christian Birth: How to give new believers a proper start in life* (Hodder and Stoughton, 1989)

# 3

# Touched by the cross

**For the message of the cross is foolishness to those who are perishing, but to us who are being saved it is the power of God.**
1 CORINTHIANS 1:18

As a young man, newly come to faith in Christ, I remember seeing a poster outside the Methodist chapel in the village where I grew up. It portrayed a silhouette of the three crosses at Calvary, and underneath were the words 'FOR YOU'. It moved me deeply, for I had only just come to know the amazing truth that when Christ died on the cross, he had died for me, so that I might be forgiven and receive eternal life.

This simple theology – that Christ died as my substitute – remains at the heart of my understanding of the cross. It is summed up for me in the words of a hymn that soon became one of my lifelong favourites: 'Bearing shame and scoffing rude, in my place condemned he stood; sealed my pardon with his blood, Hallelujah, what a Saviour' (Philip Bliss, 1838–76). Even now my heart is warmed as I write those words and consider the wonder of this Calvary love. I never want to wander from this most central and foundational truth.

The cross is far more complex than this, of course, and theologians vigorously debate its deeper meaning. However, what is important is that we come to the cross personally and receive for ourselves all the blessing that flows from that place of sacrifice. In John Bunyan's allegory *The Pilgrim's Progress*, Christian carries a great burden on his back, which is only loosed when he kneels before the cross. Each of us must likewise come to the foot of the cross, humbly and contritely, if we are to be released from our burden of guilt and shame.

Our discipleship must have the cross as its centrepiece. No matter how far we journey in following Christ, the cross must always be our touchstone. There are three crucial ways to understand the cross.

## At the cross, we are justified

To be justified is to be made right as far as the law of God is concerned, the law which rightly condemns us because of our sin. To transgress is to break the law, and all of us stand guilty and condemned before a holy God. Our sinfulness made a separation between us and God, but at the cross God made a way for us to be forgiven and made right again before the law. There at the cross, Christ took the punishment for the sins of the whole world and dealt with sin once and for all. His death was a sacrifice, making atonement for us so that we can be forgiven and made righteous before God.

This is how the apostle Paul expressed it:

> There is no difference between Jew and Gentile, for all have sinned and fall short of the glory of God, and all are justified freely by his grace through the redemption that came by Christ Jesus. God presented Christ as a sacrifice of atonement, through the shedding of his blood – to be received by faith.
> ROMANS 3:22–25

This picture, taken from the law courts, means that when we come by faith to Christ we are justified, made right forever in the eyes of God, the judge of all. The weight of guilt and shame is lifted from us because we have been forgiven, and we need never feel condemned again.

For a long time I suffered from a feeling of condemnation because I did not fully understand that all my sin was dealt with at Calvary. I continued to feel guilty and ashamed and fell prey to the accusations of Satan and feelings of unworthiness. Only when I discovered the truth of Romans 8:1 did I find freedom: 'Therefore, there is now no condemnation for those who are in Christ Jesus.' What joy, what liberty, when this truth eventually sank into my heart: no condemnation!

## Through the cross, we are reconciled

Here the picture is that of being alienated and estranged from God but then being brought back into relationship with him. Perhaps the story of the lost son in Luke 15 comes to mind. He wandered far away from home but then came to his senses and returned, impoverished and dishevelled, to be welcomed and embraced by his waiting father. This is how Paul expressed it when writing to his Gentile friends at Ephesus:

> Remember that at that time you were separate from Christ, excluded from citizenship in Israel and foreigners to the covenants of the promise, without hope and without God in the world. But now in Christ Jesus you who once were far away have been brought near by the blood of Christ.
> EPHESIANS 2:12–13

This idea of being 'brought near' opens up the possibility not only of friendship with God, but also of intimacy with him. We can banish forever from our minds any thought of a God who is distant and remote. We have been given access into his presence and are welcome there. We belong to God and have a right to draw near with boldness and confidence. It also gives us a responsibility to be reconciled to others. Christ becomes our peace, the bridge that brings us back to God and to each other.

## By the cross, we are redeemed

Now the picture is one of a slave market, where people are being bought at a price. The difference is that Christ redeems us to set us free, not to enslave us again. Having paid the ransom price at the cross, he frees us from the bondage we were under to sin and liberates us to serve God willingly and joyfully. Jesus himself spoke of his death in these terms: 'For even the Son of Man did not come to be served, but to serve, and to give his life as a ransom for many' (Mark 10:45).

This awareness of having been bought at a price is taken up by the apostle Peter. He writes:

> For you know that it was not with perishable things such as silver or gold that you were redeemed from the empty way of life handed down to you from your ancestors, but with the precious blood of Christ, a lamb without blemish or defect.
> 1 PETER 1:18–19

A hefty price was paid for our freedom, for which we are to live with a corresponding sense of gratitude. As one of the great hymns puts it:

*Were the whole realm of nature mine,*
*that were a present far too small.*
*Love so amazing, so divine,*
*demands my soul, my life, my all.*
Isaac Watts (1674–1748)

Indeed, gratitude becomes the motivation for giving ourselves to God and for living a holy life. To the believers in Corinth, often described as the Vanity Fair of the ancient world because of its licentiousness, Paul gives this exhortation: 'You are not your own; you were bought at a price. Therefore honour God with your bodies' (1 Corinthians 6:19–20). When we understand the cross and what it cost, we will find strength to live with purity in our own sex-saturated and promiscuous culture. It will give us the power we need to overcome temptation and to choose to live in the right way.

The cross then justifies us before the law, reconciles us to a Father from whom we might otherwise be estranged and sets us free from our slavery to sin so we can live a new life. No wonder believers make so much of the cross. It is the ground of our confidence and the basis for our assurance. We can say happily with the apostle Paul, 'May I never boast except in the cross of our Lord Jesus Christ, through which the world has been crucified to me, and I to the world' (Galatians 6:14).

## Conversation starters

1 When did you first hear the message of the cross? How did you respond to it? What does it mean to you now?
2 At the cross, we are justified. Why is it important to know that the law has been satisfied and that we are justified (acquitted, found not guilty) before God? If you have suffered from a sense of condemnation, how does this help you?
3 Through the cross, we are reconciled. What does it mean to you to be able to approach God with boldness and confidence? If you feel unworthy or lacking in confidence, how can this truth help you?
4 By the cross, we are redeemed. Do you feel grateful for what Christ has done for you? How can this motivate you in your battle with temptation?
5 How might regularly taking part in the Communion service strengthen your awareness of the cross?

# Helpful reading

Max Lucado, *He Chose the Nails: What God did to win your heart* (Nelson, 2000)

John Stott, *Basic Christianity* (IVP, 1958)

John Stott, *The Cross of Christ* (IVP, 1989)

Tom Wright, *The Day the Revolution Began: Reconsidering the meaning of Jesus' crucifixion* (SPCK, 2016)

# 4

# In Christ

**Therefore, if anyone is in Christ, the new creation has come: the old has gone, the new is here!**
2 CORINTHIANS 5:17

The next two chapters belong together, as they are really two sides of the same coin – the foundational truths that from God's perspective we are in Christ and that Christ is in us. This truth finds its best expression in the illustration of the vine and the branches in John 15:1–8. Christ is the vine, and we are the branches. The branches are connected to the vine (we are in Christ), and the life of the vine flows into the branches (Christ is in us). First we look at the remarkable fact that anyone who is a believer has been united with Christ, which has been described as 'a vital, organic, intimate union with Jesus Christ, including a shared life and love'.[9]

This truth of our union with Christ is a theological truth, a fact revealed to us in scripture and made real to us by the Holy Spirit. It is not something we feel, but something we believe by faith. Neither is it a relationship we achieve by our own effort or goodness, but a position we are given. It is purely an act of God, as Paul makes clear to us: 'It is because of him that you are in Christ Jesus' (1 Corinthians 1:30). This was true of the believers in Corinth even though they were weak and mixed up, and it is true of every believer today, whatever the level of their spiritual maturity. In the New Testament it is the most common way of describing a Christian – someone who is 'in Christ', 'in him' or 'in the Lord'. Such expressions are used 164 times in Paul's letters alone, and this teaching was central to the apostle's understanding of the Christian life.

What makes it possible for us to be united to Christ is that we have come to him in repentance and faith and have been born again by the Spirit (chapter 2). When this miracle of conversion takes place, many other things happen to us as well, the chief being that we are placed 'in Christ', spiritually joined to him so that we are made one with him. To the Ephesians Paul writes, 'And you also were included in Christ when you heard the message of truth, the gospel of your salvation' (Ephesians 1:13). They had been included or incorporated into Christ as a gracious act of God. This is not something they had done, but it was done for them by God himself when they responded to the gospel message in faith.

Another way of looking at this is to say that we have been transferred from one realm to another, from being 'in Adam' to being 'in Christ'. This contrast is highlighted by Paul in 1 Corinthians 15:22, where he states, 'For as in Adam all die, so in Christ all will be made alive.' If you like football, you will be aware of the transfer system by which one player may be bought by another club. When the transfer takes place, the individual no longer plays for the former club, but for the new team. We can say that we have been transferred from team Adam to team Christ.

Before our conversion we were in union with Adam by birth, sharing his fallen nature as part of a fallen humanity. When God broke into our lives to save us, he took us out of that realm and placed us, by new birth, into the realm of Christ to be part of a brand-new humanity and with a new nature. That is why we say that if anyone is in Christ they are a new creation; their old life has finished and a new one has begun (2 Corinthians 5:17).

Baptism is the public proclamation of our faith in Christ and a visual demonstration of this great truth. When we are baptised, we are baptised *into* Christ, a reminder to us of what happened at our conversion when God placed us into Christ. Thus we read, 'So in Christ Jesus you are all children of God through faith, for all of you who were baptised into Christ have clothed yourselves with Christ' (Galatians 3:26–27). It is as if the filthy rags of our own unrighteousness have been removed and we have been clothed in the pure, clean garments of Christ's righteousness.

This becomes our new status, and it gives us all equal standing before God. We become part of a new community, the fellowship of those who are together in Christ. The passage continues, 'There is neither Jew nor Gentile, neither slave nor free, nor is there male or female, for you are all one in Christ Jesus' (v. 28). All distinctions and barriers are removed when we are in Christ. Racial divisions, gender gaps and class differences disappear as we find our common ground in Christ. This is the only basis for spiritual unity.

The wonderful truth behind this understanding is that once we are 'in Christ' we are forever joined to him. The union is indissoluble. From that moment on God only ever sees us as we are in Christ, and in him we are made complete. We share his holiness and his righteousness and are completely accepted by the Father – not because we are perfect, but because we are made perfect 'in him'. John Stott writes, 'Once we are united to Jesus Christ, God the Father no longer sees us in our sins, for he sees us in Christ.'[10]

It is this understanding that gives us our confidence before God. We are bold to come before his throne, not because of our own righteousness, but because we are clothed in Christ's righteousness. We dare to draw near with boldness. We stand before God with our head held high because of who we are 'in Christ'. If the Father no longer sees us in our sin, and sees us only as we are in Christ, then that is also how we must see ourselves. We should not think of ourselves as despicable sinners nor dwell on our shortcomings and failures. Our self-esteem is to be built around who we are in Christ and what God thinks of us. We are both accepted and made acceptable. This is the place to which grace has brought us. No wonder Andrew Murray writes, 'The whole Christian life depends on the clear consciousness of our position in Christ.'[11]

Once we are in Christ, we have access to all the blessing that God has in store for us. All of God's plans and purposes find their fulfilment in him and come to us through our relationship with him. In one of the most thrilling statements in the New Testament, Paul makes this declaration: 'Blessed be the God and Father of our Lord Jesus Christ, who has blessed us in Christ with every spiritual blessing in the heavenly places' (Ephesians 1:3, RSV). He is talking about spiritual blessings, those benefits which have to do with our relationship with God, rather than material, earthly ones. The following paragraph (vv. 4–14, which is without a sentence break, such is Paul's excitement) highlights these blessings:

- becoming holy in his sight (v. 4)
- our adoption as sons (v. 5)
- the riches of his grace lavished on us (v. 6)
- redemption and forgiveness (v. 7)
- the promised Holy Spirit (v. 13).

This is no exhaustive list, but it is a good starting point as we begin to discover all that is ours in Christ.

In order to grow into this truth, we must discipline our thinking so that we continually say to ourselves, 'I am in Christ.' We must resist the temptation to think of ourselves in any other way, as if somehow we had been cut adrift from Christ and made dependent on our own righteousness. No, we are in Christ, and we are complete in him. This is our divinely given standing before God, and it will never change.

## Conversation starters

1  If a clear awareness of our position in Christ is vital to our Christian life, yet it is not something we feel, how can we be sure that we are in Christ?
2  How does being in Christ give us confidence before God? How does it change your view of yourself? Is this something you need to take hold of?
3  Why do you think being baptised as a declaration of faith in Christ is an important step in Christian discipleship? What other truths does it express?
4  Meditate on Ephesians 1:3–14. Which of the benefits listed in this passage do you need to receive into your life?
5  How might you increase your awareness that you are now in Christ?

## Helpful reading

Edward Donnelly, *Life in Christ: Walking in newness of life* (Bryntirion Press, 2007)
Tony Horsfall, *A Fruitful Life: Abiding in Christ as seen in John 15* (BRF, 2006)
Andrew Murray, *The True Vine* (Moody Press, 1997)
Warren Wiersbe, *Abide: Understanding the secrets of living for Jesus* (10 Publishing, 2016)
Bruce Wilkinson, *Secrets of the Vine: Breaking through to abundance* (Multnomah, 2001)

# 5

# Christ in me

**I pray that out of his glorious riches he may strengthen you with power through his Spirit in your inner being, so that Christ may dwell in your hearts through faith.**
EPHESIANS 3:16–17

The two central truths – that I am in Christ and that Christ is in me – are brought together beautifully by Jesus in his teaching about the vine and the branches. The branch is connected to the vine (I am in Christ), and the life of the vine flows into the branch (Christ is in me). This is the secret of the Christian life. Jesus says, 'I am the vine; you are the branches. If you remain in me and I in you, you will bear much fruit; apart from me you can do nothing' (John 15:5). In this chapter we focus on the second aspect of this great truth, reminding ourselves that Christ lives in us.

David Watson (1933–84) was an influential leader in the charismatic movement in England during the 1970s. He had taken over a near-redundant church in York and transformed it into a vital and growing congregation, and from his base there he successfully led many university missions and outreach events all over the country. On one occasion I had the privilege of hearing him speak.

During his talk, Watson took a glove and placed it on the pulpit. 'Now, glove,' he said, 'pick up that Bible.' Of course, there was no response, so he repeated the command several times, again without effect. Then he placed his hand in the glove and repeated the command, 'Glove, pick up that Bible,' this time with immediate success. His point was this: a lifeless glove cannot do what is asked of it, for it has no power. Only a glove that is animated by the life of its owner could possibly perform the task. Likewise, it is only when we are indwelt by the life of Christ that we can live the Christian life effectively. The Christian life *is* the Christ-life. Disciples are to be animated by this power within.

Just as at our conversion we are incorporated into Christ, so at the moment of the new birth the life of Christ enters into us by his Spirit. The first is a truth we accept by faith, not something we feel experientially; the second, however, is something we are soon aware of, because the Spirit makes us conscious that there is a new power within us, the life of the Son. We have seen already that we were included in Christ when we first believed. Paul goes on to say in the same verse that something else also happened: 'When you believed, you were marked in him with a seal, the promised Holy Spirit' (Ephesians 1:13). The indwelling Spirit assures us of our salvation and releases the life of Christ within us. To have the Spirit is to have the life of Christ, and this is true of every believer.

This knowledge, that Christ now lives in us, has been called 'the liberating secret'[12] because it holds the key to how we can live a victorious Christian life. The apostle Paul spoke of it as a 'mystery', not because it was deliberately kept secret but because it required faith to understand it. This was true for Jew and Gentile alike, and he writes, 'To them God has chosen to make known among the Gentiles the glorious riches of this mystery, which is Christ in you, the hope of glory' (Colossians 1:27). Christ is not just near us, but also within us. He is not simply 'out there'; he is amazingly 'in here'. He has taken up residence within every believer to make it possible for us to do the things he asks us to do.

Lloyd John Ogilvie (1931–2019) was an accomplished author, preacher and former chaplain to the United States Senate. In one of his books[13] he tells how after a few years in the ministry he was exhausted and frustrated, faultless in his doctrine and zealous in his efforts, but powerless to make a difference in people's lives. In his discouragement he asked God to show him what was wrong and was led to this very verse. Suddenly, he saw the answer to his need, got down on his knees and prayed, 'Lord, I've missed the secret. I have been ministering for you and have not allowed you to work through me. Come live your life in me. Love through me; forgive through me; suffer for the estranged through me; continue fresh realisations of Calvary everywhere about me.' The experience transformed his personal life and ministry, liberating him from his compulsive efforts to serve God in his own strength and refreshing his parched and thirsty soul.

This realisation, that Christ lives within us, has three significant consequences.

1   It means that *he gives us power for service*. Paul went on to say that his purpose in life was to present every person mature in Christ, and he found strength for this arduous task not in his own resources but through the power of Christ within him. He writes, 'To this end I strenuously contend with all the energy Christ so powerfully works in me' (Colossians 1:29). We give ourselves fully to the task God has given us, but always in dependency on Christ, allowing him to work in us and through us. This is the key to avoiding burnout and to sustaining ministry over the long haul.

2   It means that *he offers the possibility of transformation*. We are able to become like Christ because his life is within us. We become like him, not by some external imitation of a figure we admire, but by an internal sharing or participating in his life. Yes, we are called to imitate Christ (1 Corinthians 11:1), but following his example is made possible only because we share his life. This transformation is called spiritual formation, and it happens as we allow Christ to rule in our hearts. There is often a struggle, however, as Paul discovered with the Galatians: 'My dear children,' he writes, 'with whom I am again in the pains of childbirth until Christ is formed in you' (Galatians 4:19). Change is never easy, especially that which goes to the very root of our character, but it is made possible for us because we have the life of Christ within.

3   It means that *he provides the way to victory*. All of us know what it is to be tempted and tested. The devil is a relentless foe whose objective is to draw us back into a life of sin. He understands human weakness, and he knows how to attack us with his fiery darts. We need to remind ourselves that Jesus has overcome the devil and that he is able to live his victorious life in us who believe in him. He himself is the way to victory. There is no need for us to be intimidated by the power of Satan because, as the apostle John said, 'the one who is in you is greater than the one who is in the world' (1 John 4:4).

How does all this translate into ordinary life? Don't be surprised if God allows you to experience failure or brokenness. These may be painful experiences, but they have the effect of bringing home to us the reality that we cannot live the Christian life unaided. We need God's help each day because, as Jesus said, 'apart from me you can do nothing' (John 15:5). Knowing this we can make it our prayer every day to live in dependency on God and allow Christ to live his life in and through us. Ask him to give you the strength to serve, the desire to change and the confidence to stand tall against the enemy.

## Conversation starters

1  Why do you think the truth of 'Christ in you' is described as a liberating secret?
2  What do you learn from the testimony of Lloyd John Ogilvie? Why may failure, exhaustion and brokenness actually prove to be a help to us?
3  What does it mean to live in dependency on God? How is this currently expressed in your life?
4  What is the difference between imitation and participation when it comes to becoming like Christ?
5  What temptations are you facing? Do you have an Achilles heel? How can Jesus give you victory?

## Helpful reading

Tony Horsfall, *A Fruitful Life: Abiding in Christ as seen in John 15* (BRF, 2006)
Steve McVey, *Grace Walk: What you've always wanted in the Christian life* (Harvest House, 1995)
Andrew Murray, *The True Vine* (Moody Press, 1997)
Charles Price, *Christ in You* (Kingsway, 1995)
Bruce Wilkinson, *Secrets of the Vine: Breaking through to abundance* (Multnomah, 2001)

# Steps to growth

# 6

# Knowing your true identity

**See what great love the Father has lavished on us, that we should be called children of God! And that is what we are!**
1 JOHN 3:1

The question 'Who am I?' is a recurring one in the human journey. In some ways it is easy to answer – I am Tony, married to Evelyn, and I live in Yorkshire. In other ways it is much harder to articulate – who am I really, beneath my roles and outward appearances and the image I present to the world?

How we understand our identity affects how we perceive ourselves and how we see ourselves in relation to others. It affects our behaviour and ability to live life effectively. A well-formed identity gives us a sense of worth and value and is the basis for our self-confidence; a lack of clear identity lowers our self-esteem and may cause us to stumble through life less effectively. Not surprisingly, the search for our true identity is a deeply spiritual quest. The Bible says that we each have an intrinsic worth and value because we were made by God and created for relationship with him. It also says that we have inestimable value because the Son of God gave himself to die for us and redeemed us at great personal cost (1 Peter 1:18–19).

At our core we are God's deeply loved children. The whole of the Christian life is in fact a journey into the discovery of this most wonderful identity and then a taking hold of it in such a way that it shapes who we are and how we live. Yet achieving this is easier said than done, because most of us have created a false identity for ourselves based on the world's system of values. This false way of regarding ourselves can be hard to shake off, and even when we find our true identity in God we are always prone to slip back into our former way of thinking. Like a bar of soap, it can be difficult to grasp: just when we think we have it, it slips away from us again.

Why is this? We are all shaped by our family history and the society in which we live. We drink in messages about our value from other people and in particular from the media and the norms of society. To get by in the world we learn to define ourselves by the standards set for us by others, and this is how we create a false identity for ourselves, often at odds with the way God sees us. There are several common ways by which we forge an identity for ourselves apart from God.

1 *Through our performance.* From an early age we learn to please others to gain approval. If we behave acceptably we are considered 'good', and if we behave badly we are labelled 'bad'. These labels stick, and subconsciously we can go through life always trying to perform acceptably in the eyes of others and to conform to their expectations. This is the root of perfectionism and people-pleasing. Alternatively, when we fail to perform well, we see ourselves as being not good enough, inadequate and perhaps even a failure. This is the root of inferiority.

2 *Through our profession.* Work gives us a ready-made sense of identity. Who am I? I am a nurse, a teacher, a doctor and so on. Certain professions carry great kudos and boost our self-worth. Other jobs may be lower down the scale and cause us to value ourselves less than others. Of course, if our identity is tied to what we do and we lose our job, then we have an identity crisis. As someone smartly put it, 'When I do, then I am; when I don't, then I'm not.'

3 *Through our possessions.* In a materialistic world driven by consumerism, it is easy to define ourselves by 'things' – the car we drive, the clothes we wear, the place we live and so on. These are external markers of worth for many people, but totally unreliable when it comes to estimating a person's true worth. Character and dignity have nothing to do with material wealth, and we cannot be defined by mere things.

4 *Through our pleasures.* We live in a hedonistic world, where pleasure rules and experience reigns. In order to feel alive people must continue to feel 'high' – whether through drink, drugs, sex, gambling or the latest adrenalin-inducing adventure. None of these satisfy permanently; all of them give only a temporary thrill that must be repeated again until it becomes addictive. When we don't know who we are, pleasure gives a certain relief to the emptiness inside but offers no lasting clue as to our true identity.

We could easily add to this list. It is not difficult to look around and see people caught up in these false identities and unhelpful strategies for finding worth. Perhaps we can see the same forces at work in our own lives. The spiritual life is a slow journey into the understanding that I am loved unconditionally by God – known for who I am, with nothing hidden or unseen and yet loved just the same. This knowledge gives us our security and helps us become the people who God intended us to be. When we know ourselves to be deeply and eternally loved, not only are we freed to love God in return, but we are also able to love others genuinely.

Henri Nouwen (1932–96) was a priest, philosopher, writer and theologian who taught at both Yale Divinity School and Harvard University. Outwardly successful in his career, he was inwardly insecure and greatly in need of love. His identity lay firmly in his accomplishments until one day he encountered a painting entitled *The Return of the Prodigal Son* by Rembrandt (1606–69). Nouwen felt strangely drawn to the painting and began to meditate on it, and the associated story in Luke 15, over a period of time. Gradually he began to see what it was all about – coming home to love – and the transforming discovery that we are all in some way like the prodigal, because we look for love in all the wrong places.

This proved a major turning-point for the priest as he discovered his own true identity as a deeply loved child of God. From merely teaching about love he came to know himself as one loved without condition or prerequisite and found a place of peace within himself where he had not been before. He wrote:

> It is the place where I am held safe in the embrace of an all-loving Father who calls me by name and says, 'You are my beloved son, on you my favour rests.'[14]

For David Benner, a professor of psychology and spirituality in America, the journey into love is at the heart of Christian spirituality. He has said that his own struggle to become more loving has been the most discouraging aspect of his own spiritual journey, but that he finds his heart beginning to thaw as he considers the cross and the extravagant love of God for him displayed there. He writes:

> Meditating on God's love has done more to increase my love than decades of effort to try to be more loving. Allowing myself to deeply

experience his love – taking time to soak in it and allow it to infuse me – has begun to effect changes that I had given up hope of ever experiencing.[15]

For Benner, as for all of us, such transformation is part of a long and often slow journey of coming to know our identity as God's deeply loved child.

There are at least three occasions in life when the question 'Who am I?' rises to the surface, and each time we must discover again that the answer is the same: 'You are God's deeply loved child.'

1   We ask the question first in our *teenage years*, when we begin to form our own identity as distinct from that of our parents. 'Who am I in my own right?' is what we ask. We want to be different, to be our own person, and it is easy to create an identity based on peer pressure or media stereo-types, but really the true answer is: 'You are made by God, for God, and your identity is that you are his deeply loved child.' This makes each of us unique and special, with no need to copy others.

2   During *midlife* the question resurfaces with just as great a force (see chapter 27). 'Who am I outside of my job and my relationships?' we ask. 'Where is the real me to be found?' Midlife can be a dangerous phase, for, as Nouwen found, we may look for love in the wrong places. But if we are wise and get the help we need, the angst we feel can be the making of us, for we can come to see with greater clarity than ever before that our true identity is found only in God. We are his beloved children.

3   Finally, in *post-retirement* and during the later stages of life we will likely encounter the question again: 'Who am I when I am no longer productive, when I can no longer make a contribution?' Again the answer is the same: 'You are God's deeply loved child, whether you can contribute or not. You are loved as you are, for who you are.' That discovery can help us end our days in peace and contentment, but we may need to find our true identity again for a new season of life.

## Conversation starters

1 Why is the question of identity (who I really am) such a significant one?
2 How have you tried to create an identity for yourself that may not be authentic? What does it look like?
3 Why do you think the discovery of our identity as God's deeply loved children is at the heart of the Christian life?
4 What do you learn from the stories of Henri Nouwen and David Benner?
5 What stage of life are you at? How does this impact your sense of identity?

## Helpful reading

David Benner, *Surrender to Love: Discovering the heart of Christian spirituality* (IVP, 2003)
Tim Keller, *The Prodigal God: Recovering the heart of the Christian faith* (Hodder and Stoughton, 2008)
Brennan Manning, *Abba's Child: The cry of the heart for intimate belonging* (NavPress, 1994)
Henri Nouwen, *The Return of the Prodigal Son: A story of homecoming* (Darton, Longman and Todd, 1994)
James Bryan Smith, *A Little Handbook of God's Love* (Hodder and Stoughton, 1995)

# 7

# At home in the Bible

**Your word is a lamp for my feet, a light on my path.**
PSALM 119:105

The Bible presents us with the objective truth we need to build our faith on. We do not need to rely on our subjective experiences alone, because these may change over time. Neither do we need to follow the ideas and philosophies of society. God has given us a more reliable and trustworthy basis for our faith in his unchanging word.

The Bible itself is a miracle. It is really a library of 66 different books, written by more than 40 different authors over a period of around 1,500 years, yet it reads like one book with one consistent message – God's great plan of salvation and restoration. This is the unifying theme, despite it having been written at different times, in different cultures and in different languages. God has gone to great trouble to place it into our hands, and people have given their lives to pass it on to other generations and to translate it into almost every language on earth. It is a book to be valued and treasured like no other.

Most Christians believe in the inspiration of the Bible. One statement of faith speaks about 'the divine inspiration and supreme authority of the Old and New Testament Scriptures, which are the written Word of God – fully trustworthy for faith and conduct'.[16] This doesn't mean that we don't sometimes have questions about the Bible, but that we trust in its reliability even when we may not understand everything it says.

The Bible will always play a major part in the maturing of our faith, enlightening our understanding, informing our decisions and strengthening our beliefs. It will shape how we think, determine the way we live and help to form our character. Here are some ways by which we can benefit from the Bible as we seek to grow in our discipleship.

1   *Read the Bible from cover to cover*, as many times as possible over the course of your lifetime. Get to know its story, from Genesis to Revelation. This requires great perseverance, for it is not always an easy book to read, but regular systematic Bible reading will pay rich dividends in your understanding of God and his ways. The Bible is interrelated within itself, so understanding one part is helpful for knowing the other parts. The Old Testament has to be seen in the light of the New Testament, but the New Testament cannot be understood without a knowledge of the Old. The more we get to know the Bible, the greater will be our appreciation for it. Although I have been reading it steadily now for more than 50 years, and I would say I have a good grasp of scripture, I still wish I had read it more.

2   *Get to know the big picture of the Bible*, the overarching themes and how it all hangs together. Understanding the whole will help you understand the parts. There are many overviews of the Bible, but *The Bible Course*,[17] an eight-part DVD course presented by Andrew Ollerton, is particularly helpful. Using a unique storyline, the course shows how the key events, books and characters all fit together. It helps participants to read the Bible for themselves and builds confidence in understanding and interpreting the Bible, as well as applying its message to daily life. Having a strategic grasp of the Bible is key to being at home in its pages.

3   *Become familiar with the lives of the men and women of faith* whose stories are told in the Bible – people like Abraham and Moses, Joseph and Joshua, Deborah and Esther, King David, Peter and Paul and so on. Their lives are laid bare before us so that we can learn from their experiences, both good and bad. They become examples for us, showing us how to live well and warning us of pitfalls to be avoided. They become companions to us on our spiritual journey, people of old who become our friends today. As Paul puts it, 'Everything that was written in the past was written to teach us, so that through the endurance taught in the Scriptures and the encouragement they provide we might have hope' (Romans 15:4).

4   *Let it speak to you personally*, not just informing your mind but moving your will to action. The Bible is a living book, and God speaks to us through it, therefore we should always read it with an attentive heart. This is why the Bible is so unique. Not only do we read it, but the Bible also reads us, revealing what is in our hearts (Hebrews 4:12–13). We do not sit in judgement on God's word; it sits in judgement on us. Paul encourages the young leader Timothy to be familiar with the scriptures, saying:

All Scripture is God-breathed and is useful for teaching, rebuking, correcting and training in righteousness, so that the servant of God may be thoroughly equipped for every good work.
2 TIMOTHY 3:16–17

Think of it like this:

- *Teaching*: the Bible sets us on the right path, the way of truth and wisdom.
- *Rebuking*: it shows us when we are going astray and when we are doing wrong.
- *Correcting*: it points us in the right direction again and shows us how to put things right.
- *Training*: it helps us to establish new patterns of thought and behaviour, so we can keep walking in the right path.

This constant interaction with the Bible over time is what leads to our transformation. When we allow the word of God to dwell in us richly (Colossians 3:16, RSV), it begins to impact positively on every aspect of our life.

One of the most enjoyable ways of reading the Bible is the practice of *lectio divina*, a discipline practised in the church for nearly 1,500 years. It was introduced by Benedict (480–550) as a way of encouraging his followers to listen to God through scripture. It is a devotional approach rather than an academic one, whereby we simply allow the words of scripture to address us personally. It is mostly used in a group setting, and the method is quite simple:

1 A short passage is chosen and read aloud slowly, perhaps twice. Each person listens attentively for a word or phrase that seems to be given to them, attracts their attention or stands out to them. This then becomes the word they take forward and meditate upon, believing that it is God who has drawn their attention to it.

2 The passage is then read aloud again, slowly, and people are given time to see their word in its context again but also to prayerfully ask the questions, 'Why has this word been given to me? How does it connect with my life at this particular time?'

3 Then the passage is read a fourth time, again slowly and meditatively. This time space is given to meditate on the question, 'How does God want

me to respond to this word?' Is there a promise to receive or a warning to heed? Is there something to give thanks for or to pray further about?

4   After a time of silent prayer, opportunity can be given to share with the group what has been received. Then a closing prayer concludes the exercise. Often a word received in this way can stay with us for a long time, and it can be helpful to journal about it later to get the full meaning of what God has said.

The great value of *lectio divina* is that it offers a way by which God can speak directly to us, often taking us by surprise and bypassing our defences. It also provides a level playing field for hearing the voice of God, since those new to the faith can take part as well as those who are already well-taught.

## Conversation starters

1   What part has the Bible played in your spiritual formation so far? How has it helped you? How has it challenged you?
2   What is your normal practice of engaging with scripture? Are you satisfied with this? How might you improve on what you already do?
3   Who is your favourite Bible character, and why? What have you learnt from their story?
4   Are there any issues about the Bible that you would like to discuss?
5   If you are already familiar with *lectio divina*, how have you found this practice? If not, why not try it out?

## Helpful reading

Andy Croft and Mike Pilavachi, *Storylines: Your map to understanding the Bible* (David C. Cook, 2010)
Richard Foster, *Life with God: A life-transforming new approach to Bible reading* (Hodder and Stoughton, 2008)
M. Robert Mulholland Jr, *Shaped by the Word: The power of scripture in spiritual formation* (Upper Room Books, 2000)
Amy Orr-Ewing, *Why Trust the Bible? Answers to 10 tough questions* (IVP, 2005)
Richard Peace, *Contemplative Bible Reading: Experiencing God through scripture* (NavPress, 1998)

# 8

# Life in the Spirit

**Since we live by the Spirit, let us keep in step with the Spirit.**
GALATIANS 5:25

The Holy Spirit is the third member of the Trinity, and his work is to help us to serve God effectively and become more like Jesus. Spiritual growth is dependent on a deep and growing relationship with the Spirit, which is the subject of this chapter. However, it is impossible to cover the amazing ministry of the Spirit in one short chapter, so we will of necessity be 'skating on the surface' of all that the Bible has to say. Added to this, among believers there are different understandings of the work of the Spirit, so I can only give here my own thoughts, inadequate as they may be. What is vital is not so much having a perfect analysis of Bible teaching but a living experience of the power of the Spirit in our lives.

Jesus promised his disciples that when he returned to the Father he would not leave them as orphans, but would send to them the Holy Spirit to be their helper or counsellor. As such he would draw alongside them to teach them, guide them and empower them for witness (John 14:15–17; 15:26–27; 16:7–11). At Pentecost the Holy Spirit was poured out upon the disciples gathered in the upper room in fulfilment of this promise (Acts 2:1–4), and since that day he has continued to be available to the church. The book of Acts describes how the Spirit helped the first believers to take the gospel from Jerusalem to Rome, and he has been at work in and through God's people ever since. Three key words describe his ongoing ministry towards believers: sealed, filled and anointed.

## Sealed

At the moment of our conversion we receive the gift of the Spirit. It is impossible to come to faith without his ministry, since he is the one who draws us to Christ. But it is also impossible to live the new life without his help. When we come to Christ, we are *sealed* with the Spirit; that is, he comes to dwell inside us and to mark us out as belonging to God (Ephesians 1:13–14; 4:30; 2 Corinthians 1:21–22; Acts 2:38–39). As a result we experience an assurance that we are now God's children and that God is in fact our heavenly Father (Romans 8:15–16). This provides us with a solid foundation on which to grow in grace. Every believer has the Holy Spirit. This is something we believe, not something to which we must attain.

## Filled

However, the fact that we have received the Holy Spirit is only the start of our relationship with him. The next step is to be *filled* with the Spirit, to allow him to lead and guide us and to live in submission to his direction. Paul makes this abundantly clear in one of the most important commands in the Bible: 'Be filled with the Spirit' (Ephesians 5:18). This is an ongoing command, so that the continuous state of the believer is to be living in dependence on the Spirit and in obedience to his promptings. This is to be our way of life, and our progress will be hindered unless we keep our relationship with the Spirit in good repair.

Being filled with the Spirit for the first time is sometimes referred to as being baptised in the Spirit, as it is an initial experience. Baptism in the Spirit occurs only once, but being filled with the Spirit is a continuous experience. Thus on the day of Pentecost the disciples were baptised in the Spirit (Acts 1:5), but they were also filled with the Spirit both then and subsequently (Acts 2:4; 4:8, 31; 6:5; 9:17; 13:9). Sometimes the baptism of the Spirit is accompanied by clear indicators of a supernatural encounter, through specific gifts like speaking in tongues, prophecy or an overwhelming sense of being loved by God and being bathed in his presence (Acts 10:44–46; 19:6). At other times it may be quiet but just as real; we know with assurance that he is within our hearts, and our faith is strengthened as a result.

## Anointed

Even this does not exhaust the range of the ministry of the Spirit towards us. One of the major ways he assists us is to *anoint* us for service; that is, to empower us for specific tasks as and when we need his help. Jesus himself operated in this way, declaring in the synagogue at Nazareth: 'The Spirit of the Lord is on me, because he has anointed me to proclaim good news to the poor' (Luke 4:18; see also Acts 10:38). The anointing of the Spirit is always for a specific task, and it represents a 'coming upon' us by the Holy Spirit, giving us a boldness or ability we may not otherwise have. This is the kind of help we need whenever we are preaching or teaching, witnessing to others, serving the poor and needy and so on. It reflects both our dependency upon God and our confidence that he will give us the power we need when we need it (Luke 24:49).

When we consistently live a life in the Spirit, we discover that two things happen.

1   The Holy Spirit begins to change us from the inside out, producing in us the beautiful fruit of the Spirit, which is a visible expression of the life of Christ – love, joy, peace, patience, kindness, goodness, faithfulness, gentleness and self-control (Galatians 5:22–23). This is what holiness looks like, and it is attractive and desirable, not austere and unreachable.

2   He begins to impart to us supernatural gifts so that we can be effective in our service for God both inside and outside of church. This is the Spirit's work of equipping. These gifts range from moments of insight and words of wisdom to gifts of teaching and hospitality. There is a broad spectrum of such gifts, which are outlined in passages like 1 Corinthians 12:7–11, Romans 12:4–8 and 1 Peter 4:9–11. Both natural gifts (those we are born with) and spiritual gifts (those given following our new birth) come from God and are to be used with humility and gratitude to bring glory to him and for the benefit of others.

In order to live consistently in harmony with the Spirit, we are to cultivate carefully our relationship with him through prayer and waiting on God. There are three dangers we must avoid:

1   *Resisting* the Spirit (Acts 7:51), which happens when we refuse to respond to the Spirit's conviction or constraint but instead become stubborn and rebellious. It is like we are deaf to the voice of God.

2   *Grieving* the Spirit (Ephesians 4:30), which happens when we harbour sin in our lives, such as bitterness, unforgiveness or anger. It is like the channel is blocked.

3  *Quenching* the Spirit (1 Thessalonians 5:19), which happens when we are moved to act or speak by the Spirit but hold back out of fear or unbelief. It is like driving with the handbrake on.

While the Holy Spirit is as sensitive as a dove, he is not overly sensitive. We need not fear that he is easily driven away, because he is not, but we must learn to walk in fellowship with him and not take his presence for granted.

When Jesus spoke about the Spirit, he used a particular word to describe him: the Greek word *parakletos*, which means one who draws gently alongside to bring help and consolation (John 14:16). The Holy Spirit never forces his way into our lives but waits to be invited. When we recognise our need of his help and turn to him in that need, he graciously draws alongside us to bring that help. His work in our lives is clearly indispensable, which is why we must daily be filled with the Spirit.

## Conversation starters

1  Can you remember your first encounter with the Holy Spirit? What happened?
2  What has been your experience of the Holy Spirit so far?
3  How do you personally understand the baptism in the Spirit?
4  How do you know when you are filled with the Spirit? What evidence is there in your life of the fruit of the Spirit or his gifts?
5  What might inhibit the flow of the Spirit in and through your life? How can you stay in close harmony with him?

## Helpful reading

Francis Chan, *Forgotten God: Reversing our tragic neglect of the Holy Spirit* (David C. Cook, 2019)
Gordon Fee, *Paul, the Spirit, and the People of God* (Baker Academic, 1996)
R. T. Kendall, *Holy Fire: A balanced, biblical look at the Holy Spirit's work in our lives* (Charisma House, 2014)
Mike Pilavachi and Andrew Croft, *Everyday Supernatural: Living a Spirit-led life without being weird* (David C. Cook, 2016)
Simon Ponsonby, *God Inside Out: An in-depth study of the Holy Spirit* (Kingsway, 2007)

# 9

# Changing patterns of prayer

**And pray in the Spirit on all occasions with all kinds of prayers and requests. With this in mind, be alert and always keep on praying for all the Lord's people.**
EPHESIANS 6:18

Prayer is the instinctive response of the human heart to trouble, a cry to God for help. Even atheists pray when they are in a tight corner. Prayer is so simple that a child can do it, and yet so profound that the greatest theologians cannot fully comprehend how it works. It remains a mystery, and yet prayer is one of God's greatest gifts to us – the ability to communicate directly with him.

Prayer is the first sign of new life. When Ananias was sent to encourage Saul after his conversion, he was told, 'Behold, he is praying' (Acts 9:11, RSV). Learning how to pray is one of our first lessons in Christian discipleship. It is often summarised by the acronym ACTS – adoration, confession, thanksgiving and supplication. These four types of prayer become the foundation of the devotional life, to which we can add intercession (praying for the needs of others). We learn how to pray alone (personal prayer) and with others (corporate prayer); how to pray audibly (extempore prayer) and in unison (liturgical prayer). Above all we are encouraged to let our requests be made known to God and expect that he will hear us (Philippians 4:6). Thus a life of prayer becomes the bedrock of a healthy walk with God.

Most of us will have known many answers to prayer, sufficient to convince us that prayer does work. Yet we also experience times when prayers are seemingly not answered. We struggle to find the right formula so that our prayers hit the mark consistently. We may intensify our prayers (adding fasting, increasing the length of our prayers, upping the volume) or increase their purity (more faith, greater holiness, praying in tongues), but often with no greater control over the outcome. Perhaps we are introduced to the idea of prayer as spiritual warfare, and we learn how to bind and to loose demonic powers, praying with greater authority. But always prayer remains somewhat elusive. No wonder that there seems to be more Christian books written about prayer than any other topic.

The desire to determine the outcome of prayer seems to be at the heart of our struggle. We may unconsciously use prayer as a way of controlling the world. Without realising, we slip into an understanding of prayer that is about getting God to do our will, rather than asking that God's will may come to pass. Our 'demandingness' becomes an issue. We expect God to do what we think is best and blame him when things don't work out as we would like. This fault line in our understanding of prayer is often exposed when we experience a major unanswered prayer – a loved one who dies rather than being healed; children who wander from the faith; a job interview that is unsuccessful; a business that fails; the inability to have children; and so on. Events like these can become stumbling blocks to our faith and make us want to quit altogether.

Such moments of despair can become major turning points if we allow them to shape us. They can throw us back upon God so that we begin to see prayer from his perspective, and we can discover new ways of praying. Our experience of prayer evolves, and it is normal for our prayer life to change and develop over time. Here are some points about maturing in prayer.

1   At some point we come to accept that there is a degree of mystery in prayer. There is no magic formula that guarantees we get what we want. Praying is not like rubbing Aladdin's lamp and then expecting God to do our bidding. A mature understanding of prayer involves a reorientation towards first of all praying according to God's will. As the apostle John says, 'This is the confidence we have in approaching God: that if we ask anything according to his will, he hears us' (1 John 5:14). Even Jesus qualified his prayer in Gethsemane with the rider, 'may your will be done' (Matthew 26:42). Gradually we learn to stop using prayer to control our world.

2   We can ask for the help of the Holy Spirit in guiding how we pray and what we ask for. In Romans 8:26, Paul reminds us that 'we do not know what we ought to pray for', but also says that 'the Spirit helps us in our weakness'. Our experience of the first makes way for the second. Once we acknowledge our inability in prayer, the Holy Spirit can begin to teach us how to pray. Indeed, he can pray through us with 'wordless groans', interpreting

our longings to God when our words are inadequate. This may well be our introduction to silent prayer, a form of prayer that is no longer based on words or our understanding, but simply being before God in stillness.

3   A next step in a deepening prayer life may be when, having realised that we do not need to act as God's advisor in all matters pertaining to the universe, we learn to simply 'hold' people and situations before God in a form of what we may call trusting prayer. We can place them into his loving care and infinite wisdom by naming them before him and then resting in his wisdom and sovereign power, giving over the outcome to him. This takes a lot of weight off human shoulders and places the government where it truly belongs – on God's shoulders (Isaiah 9:6).

4   The journey in prayer, however, does not end here. We may also find that as our awareness of God's love for us increases and our love for him grows, we are drawn into what is often called contemplative prayer. This can take two forms. First, it may be the *prayer of loving attentiveness*, where we are content to be silent before God and to bask in his love for us. This is the communion of lovers, and words are unnecessary. It is perhaps what David spoke about: 'that I may dwell in the house of the Lord all the days of my life, to gaze on the beauty of the Lord and to seek him in his temple' (Psalm 27:4). Here we are able to rest in God's presence without words, thoughts or mental images.

Alongside this, our communion with God may grow into *listening prayer*, where we begin to recognise the still, small voice of God that Elijah heard at Horeb (1 Kings 19:12). When God speaks like this, it is with the whisper of love, reminding us how deeply we are loved and establishing our identity as his deeply loved children. He may also speak with quiet words of reassurance or guidance, gently directing us into his ways. This kind of prayer becomes increasingly important as we seek to be led by the Spirit and to base our activities on the direction of God, not simply on opportunity or need.

Viewed in this light, prayer can be seen as something of an unfolding adventure. Our understanding of prayer deepens over time and reflects a growing intimacy with God. The ACTS model remains foundational, but as we grow in our faith we move way beyond that to the deeper forms of prayer that are the expression of a passionate love for God. This may require us to spend more time with God in stillness, silence and solitude. This may be costly, but it is a price worth paying.

## Conversation starters

1 What answers to prayer have you experienced? How have they encouraged your faith?
2 What difficulties have you encountered in prayer? What might God be teaching you about prayer at the moment?
3 Do you recognise the temptation to use prayer as a way of controlling your world? What is the alternative?
4 As you reflect on the stages of prayer described here, where do you think you are on your prayer journey?
5 How can you deepen your prayer life? How might a growing intimacy with God affect the way you pray?

## Helpful reading

John Dalrymple, *Simple Prayer* (Darton, Longman and Todd, 1984)
Richard Foster, *Prayer: Finding the heart's true home* (Hodder and Stoughton, 1992)
Pete Greig, *How to Pray: A simple guide for normal people* (Hodder and Stoughton, 2019)
Joyce Huggett, *Listening to God* (Hodder and Stoughton, 2016)
Philip Yancey, *Prayer: Does it make any difference?* (Hodder and Stoughton, 2006)

# 10

# Developing a servant heart

**Tychicus, the dear brother and faithful servant in the Lord.**
EPHESIANS 6:21

In many cultures of the world the role of a servant is despised. Servants are looked down upon and considered inferior, to be of a lower class. No wonder there is often an aversion towards the call to serve, even though that call permeates the Bible and is a key marker of mature discipleship. Many believers are happy to attend church, but they don't want to get involved when it comes to serving others through the ministry of the church. They feel their lives are busy enough already, and they are resistant to any invitation to get more involved.

And yet we follow one whose identity was clearly that of a servant. Jesus himself said that 'even the son of Man did not come to be served, but to serve, and to give his life as a ransom for many' (Mark 10:45). He beautifully fulfilled the picture of the servant of the Lord in Isaiah, and in particular the notion of being a suffering servant (Isaiah 42:1–9; 49:1–6; 50:4–9; 52:13—53:12). In the words of the ancient Christian hymn quoted by the apostle Paul, 'he made himself nothing by taking the very nature of a servant, being made in human likeness' (Philippians 2:7). His earthly life and ministry were lived as a servant, doing the will of God, helping those in need and eventually giving his life so that others might be saved.

Furthermore, he schooled his disciples to become servants too. He taught them that they were not to imitate the leadership style of those around them, which so often involved lording it over others. Neither should they seek to be the greatest in the group. Rather, Jesus said that the one who rules should be like the one who serves, because 'I am among you as one who serves' (Luke 22:27). During their final meal together in the upper room, Jesus took a towel and a basin of water and washed his disciples' feet, a humble act of service that set an example for them and for all his followers. 'Now that

I, your Lord and Teacher, have washed your feet,' he said, 'you also should wash one another's feet' (John 13:14).

A servant is one who is able to put the needs of others before their own. This is a sign not only of psychological and emotional maturity, but also of spiritual growth. To live a life focused solely on ourselves and our own needs is to live in a very small and narrow world; to expand our horizons to be concerned for others liberates us to become better people who are more fulfilled and satisfied. This principle is championed by the apostle Paul. 'Do nothing out of selfish ambition or vain conceit,' he writes. 'Rather, in humility value others above yourselves, not looking to your own interests but each of you to the interests of others' (Philippians 2:3–4). His young protégé Timothy is singled out as an example of this: 'I have no one else like him, who will show genuine concern for your welfare. For everyone looks out for their own interests, not those of Jesus Christ' (Philippians 2:20–21).

The call to serve is for all who would truly follow Jesus, and it has three dimensions.

1  We are to *serve God*, which is our highest calling. We are to invest our lives in doing his will and being involved in kingdom ministry. True conversion results in a focus not on personal ambition but on glorifying God. The believers in Thessalonica were a model for others in this regard, since they had 'turned to God from idols to serve the living and true God' (1 Thessalonians 1:9). Conversion brings a shift in the centre of gravity in our lives, from a focus on self to a focus on God and others. Such a change happens gradually and over time. This is the upward dimension to our service.

2  We are called to *serve each other* in the body of Christ. We are to make our gifts, talents and resources available to others, and we are to play our part in the work and ministry of the church. This is how the body grows to be vibrant and healthy. Paul reminded the believers in Galatia not to use their freedom in Christ selfishly but rather to live sacrificially: 'You, my brothers and sisters, were called to be free. But do not use your freedom to indulge the flesh; rather, serve one another humbly in love' (Galatians 5:13). No local church can function properly unless its members are committed to the principle of servant ministry and willingly make their contribution to the life of the fellowship. This is the inward dimension to our service.

3   We are also called to *serve the world*, that is, the community in which we live. We do this when we involve ourselves in helping others, being good neighbours and taking our role as citizens seriously. We do it when we share the gospel with others and when we take part in social justice projects, such as helping refugees, caring for the homeless, feeding the poor and so on. This thought is behind the parable of the good Samaritan (Luke 10:25–37), which answers the question 'Who is my neighbour?' with 'Anyone who is in need.' The Samaritan is commended because he showed mercy and gave practical assistance to the man who had been attacked. The teaching of Jesus is crystal clear: 'Go and do likewise' (v. 37). This is the outward dimension to our service.

Discipleship requires that we learn how to serve others, to be more aware of their needs and to be less wrapped up in our own concerns. This inevitably involves a death to self, something most of us strive to avoid. It is not that we have no legitimate needs of our own, for we cannot care for others unless we care for ourselves. The point is that we must be outward-looking, not self-absorbed. Richard Foster suggests there is a subtle distinction between choosing to serve and being a servant. He writes, 'When we choose to serve, we are still in charge. We decide whom we will serve and when we will serve... But when we choose to be a servant we give up our right to be in charge.'[18]

A notable characteristic of Christian ministry is that leadership should always be servant leadership. What this means is that the motivation for leadership is to serve others, not to fulfil any need we may have for power or position. Christian leaders are called to use their gift of leadership with a servant heart, looking to glorify God and to be of help to his people. When this foundation is securely in place, churches and Christian organisations will be less prone to abusive leadership or damaging patterns of discipleship. The culture will be one of humility, not pride; of self-effacement, not self-display.

We must not think, though, that servant leadership is by definition weak leadership. Some fear that if they are servants first and leaders second, they will be taken advantage of or treated as a doormat. Servant leaders are humble in their attitude and gentle in their approach, but they are no less clear in their leadership. They are not afraid to exercise authority, but they do so cautiously and with restraint. They are equally as visionary, but they do not impose their vision on others or manipulate their followers into taking part. They can be assertive when necessary and courageous when required, but always they seek to act in love.

When faced with so many needs around us, it is easy for those with servant hearts to become driven and pushed into overdrive, becoming so busy that we lose our relationship with God or suffer burnout. It is important that we practise self-care, set realistic boundaries and know our own limitations. We must only do those things that God is asking us to do, and then work not in our own strength but in dependency on God. We cannot meet every need, and we can't do everything, but we can do something. What is important is to discern what God would have us do, and then do it joyfully and with a willing heart, remembering the exhortation of the apostle Paul: 'Never be lacking in zeal, but keep your spiritual fervour, serving the Lord' (Romans 12:11).

## Conversation starters

1  What is your own attitude towards the idea of being a servant? What has your culture taught you?
2  Why is the development of a servant heart crucial for our spiritual development and effectiveness in ministry? How can we cultivate a servant heart?
3  How are you expressing the three dimensions of service described here in your life?
4  What is your understanding of servant leadership? Why is it not the same as weak leadership?
5  How can you care for yourself as well as be available to serve the needs of others?

## Helpful reading

Eddie Gibbs, *Way to Serve: Leading through serving and enabling* (IVP, 2003)
John Hindley, *Serving without Sinking: How to serve Christ and keep your joy* (The Good Book Company, 2013)
Tony Horsfall, *Servant Ministry: A portrait of Christ and a pattern for his followers* (BRF, 2013)
J. David Lundy, *Servant Leadership For Slow Learners* (Authentic, 2002)
Chuck Swindoll, *Improving Your Serve: The art of unselfish living* (W Publishing, 1981)

# Living out your faith

# 11

# Faith at work

**Daniel so distinguished himself among the chief ministers and the satraps by his exceptional qualities that the king planned to set him over the whole kingdom.**
DANIEL 6:3

It used to be that churches focused their attention almost entirely on what happened on Sundays when they met together, and that spirituality was measured by how involved members were in church activities. Thankfully such attitudes have almost disappeared now, and there is a greater emphasis on preparing and supporting people in their working lives. The sacred–secular divide is less pronounced, and there is a widespread acceptance that we serve God as much when we are at work as we do at church.

Work itself is a good thing, and the Bible encourages us to be hard-working and to provide for our families by earning a living. The apostle Paul, who combined his ministry with the work of tentmaking so as not to be a burden on others, was particularly strong on this point (2 Thessalonians 3:6–10). He set an example of hard work for others to follow, warned them against being idle and set them this principle: 'The one who is unwilling to work shall not eat' (v. 10). Perhaps this is the origin of the Protestant work ethic, the belief that we glorify God by working hard, being productive and avoiding laziness.

There are many examples of people in the Bible who served God through their work. Jesus himself was a carpenter. Peter and some of the other disciples were fishermen. We read of Joseph serving Pharaoh, of Nehemiah being cupbearer to the king and of Daniel serving in the king's palace in Babylon. Lydia was an international businesswoman from Thyatira who worked in Philippi and was instrumental in establishing a church in her home. Aquila and Priscilla travelled the Mediterranean world as tentmakers, making disciples as they went.

What this tells us is that our work can be seen as ministry, and our job can be our vocation. This dramatically changes how we view our working lives and reminds us that we can serve God fruitfully in the workplace as much as anywhere else. We are all in 'full-time' Christian ministry. Hence it is important that we seek God to guide us as to our career choice and our particular place of work. Each potential change of job should be submitted to his will for us. As we grow in our understanding of our gifting, skills and passion, and prayerfully seek to be in the place of God's choosing, we discover our vocation. This is summed up beautifully for us by Frederick Buechner: 'The place God calls you to is the place where your deep gladness and the world's deep hunger meet.'[19]

With this in mind we can now look at the practicalities of being a Christian at work. The main passages for this are in Ephesians 6:5–9 and Colossians 3:22—4:1. Here Paul shows us that our discipleship is to be worked out in our everyday lives – faith must be applied to every situation in which we find ourselves. He is writing to those who were household servants and who, while still bound to their masters, carried a degree of freedom and responsibility in their work. The situation is not exactly the same as being under an employment contract today, but the principles he expounds readily apply to the workplace now.

His starting point is to encourage all to see that they do their work out of reverence for Christ, as if they are serving him and not simply an earthly boss – 'it is the Lord Christ you are serving' (Colossians 3:24). This means that they will be cooperative and helpful, working sincerely from the heart and not just to make a good impression. They will be wholehearted and enthusiastic, aware that God sees what they do and will reward them. The implication is that they will be hard-working and seeking for excellence in all they do – 'Whatever you do, work at it with all your heart, as working for the Lord' (Colossians 3:23).

With such a positive attitude it is no wonder that God's people often find themselves in positions of leadership at work and managing other people. Again, their leadership style is to be inspired and shaped by their faith. They are to be servant leaders. They are to treat those under them fairly and with justice and to avoid being overbearing or domineering because of their position. One day leaders too will give account to their master in heaven (Ephesians 6:9; Colossians 4:1).

A major concern for many believers is how to share their faith at work. An Evangelical Alliance survey in England suggested that 53% of Christians think they would get into trouble if they shared their beliefs in a professional context. This leads to a reticence to be known as a Christian at work and for some to lead a double life, hiding from others a part of their life that means so much to them. Journalist Helen Coffey has spoken about 'coming out' at work as a Christian but also about the difficulty of being known as an openly practising Christian.[20] The fear of being treated differently, ridiculed or even getting into trouble causes many believers to keep quiet about their faith.

By contrast, we can live out Christian values in the workplace by being honest and reliable, hard-working and diligent, loyal and cooperative. Avoiding workplace gossip is important, as is being drawn into cliques. We don't want to be 'holier than thou' in our approach or judgemental in our attitude towards others who have a very different lifestyle from our own. We can achieve this by being friendly, fun to be with and interested in the lives of others and by listening well. The workplace is like a mission field, and we must make cultural adaptations without compromising our truth. At the same time, when the opportunity arises, we can with great sensitivity share something of our story with others. We mustn't go beyond what the other person is comfortable with, but we can respond to their questions in a way that is natural and unforced. The apostle Peter wrote to believers who were experiencing persecution for their faith to encourage them in living godly lives even in a pagan society. His advice seems appropriate for today:

> Always be prepared to give an answer to everyone who asks you to give the reason for the hope that you have. But do this with gentleness and respect, keeping a clear conscience, so that those who speak maliciously against your good behaviour in Christ may be ashamed of their slander.
>
> 1 PETER 3:15–16

Notice two things here: their boldness and their sensitivity. If we keep these qualities in balance, we'll be able to maintain a credible witness even at work, and if our words have been backed up by our lives, it will be effective as well.

For some people the main issue will be maintaining a work–life balance, especially those in demanding jobs. Here we must be careful that we are not being motivated by financial greed or personal ambition and pressed into burning the candle at both ends simply to have a better lifestyle or to get ahead. But when the demands placed on us are legitimate ones, we must set in place self-care strategies to ensure we do not burn out, get sick or lose our walk with God. Nowadays, enlightened employers realise the value of health and well-being, so taking care not to work ridiculous hours for extended periods, making sure we have proper holidays and having interests outside of work are all acceptable strategies to put in place. Even pacing ourselves during the working day can help – for example, making sure that we have a proper lunch break or time for a coffee or that we work from home occasionally.

It is vital that local churches support their members in their working lives. Share with others at church about what you do and the pressures you are under and ask for prayer. Perhaps find someone more experienced in the working world to be a mentor to you. If there are other believers at your workplace, why not form a prayer group for mutual support and encouragement?

## Conversation starters

1  How are you managing to integrate your faith into your working life? What are your joys? What are your challenges?
2  Do you see your work as being part of God's will for you? How might your attitude to work be different if you saw it as your vocation?
3  How is your work–life balance? What strategies do you have in place to help you live and work wisely?
4  How do you discern God's will when it comes to changing jobs or considering promotions?
5  Are you living distinctively at work? Do you find it easy to share your faith?

## Helpful reading

Ken Costa, *God at Work: Live each day with purpose* (Word, 2016)
Mark Greene, *Thank God it's Monday: Flourishing in your workplace* (Muddy Pearl, 2019)
Tony Horsfall, *Working from a Place of Rest: Jesus and the key to sustaining ministry* (BRF, 2010)
Timothy Keller, *Every Good Endeavour: Connecting your work to God's work* (Hodder and Stoughton, 2012)
Paul Valler, *Get a Life: Winning choices for working people* (IVP, 2008)

# 12

# Singleness

**Marriage isn't for everyone. Some, from birth seemingly, never give marriage a thought. Others never get asked – or accepted. And some decide not to get married for kingdom reasons.**
MATTHEW 19:12 (MSG)

For some, the call to discipleship may involve remaining single. This is a big challenge in our society, where marriage is often promoted as being the norm, and in the church, where there is an exaggerated emphasis on family life.

Most of us grow up with the assumption that one day we will find a life partner, settle down and raise a family, so if this doesn't happen in the way we expect, we may well be thrown into confusion and our faith may be tested. At the same time, some who have been married find themselves being single again through divorce or bereavement. They have to work out what singleness looks like for them while rebuilding their lives. For a few, who describe themselves as 'same-sex attracted', the choice to remain single is taken because they feel it is biblically the right thing to do. However it comes about, the single life is not one that many people would necessarily choose for themselves, nor is it always understood by others.

For believers who take discipleship seriously, there is always the possibility of staying single. If we believe that it is best to be married to someone who shares our faith and not to be 'unequally yoked', that will limit our options (2 Corinthians 6:14–15). In most churches there is a gender imbalance, with far more women than men, meaning there is even less choice of a life partner for female disciples. This makes the cost of discipleship very real indeed.

The biblical teaching that sex should be kept within the marriage relationship means that single people are called to work out their commitment to Christ by swimming against the tide of a sex-saturated world. Casual sex is the norm. People who aren't Christians may be happy to be single but are bewildered by abstinence from sex, which is regarded as at best slightly odd and at worst an abnormality. This is the challenge faced by many highly gifted, highly motivated disciples. Not surprisingly it is a source of much heartache and struggle for them.

How shall we understand the single life? We should see that it is a noble life indeed. After all, Jesus was a single man and thereby endorsed the value and credibility of being single for the sake of the gospel. The apostle Paul also seems to have been unmarried, and deliberately so, in order to give himself fully to the purpose of God for his life as an apostle to the Gentiles (1 Corinthians 7:7). When we look at the history of the church, some of its greatest figures have remained unmarried. For example, the late Anglican leader John Stott chose not to marry so that he could fulfil his calling as a minister, writer and itinerant Bible teacher. The work of the modern mission movement has been made possible only by the self-sacrifice of many single workers – it is estimated that 60% of western mission personnel in the past 200 years have been single women.[21] Being single is neither an affliction to be pitied nor an inferior status to be patronised. We should highly honour those who out of allegiance to Christ find themselves living a single life.

1  Some people are *willingly single*. They do not feel any pressure to be married and find their fulfilment in the joy of serving Christ. They recognise that there are advantages in not being burdened by the responsibility of having a spouse and a family. Such people often have the gift of celibacy, which Jesus spoke about in Matthew 19:12, where he describes 'those who choose to live like eunuchs for the sake of the kingdom of heaven'. Many of those in religious orders take a vow of celibacy and are committed to being single so they can pursue a life of prayer and service. Others recognise the weight of the apostle Paul's words that those who marry will face many additional troubles in life (1 Corinthians 7:28). Unmarried men can be more passionate about 'the Lord's affairs' and pleasing God, while unmarried women can also focus on being 'devoted to the Lord' without distraction (1 Corinthians 7:32–35). They may still be open to the possibility of marriage, but their primary concern is to give themselves to serving God without reservation. It is a choice they make freely and willingly.

2  A second group are *contentedly single*; that is, they would like to be married, and still hope for that, but have accepted the present reality of their singleness and simply get on with living life to the full. It is not easy for them to remain unmarried, but they choose not to wallow in

self-pity or give way to resentment. Instead they find grace from God to live joyfully despite their feelings of loneliness or desire for a specific type of love and family. They have worked through the questions around their singleness and accepted it as God's will for them at this moment in time, choosing to give themselves wholeheartedly to the people whom God has placed around them. They do not feel this is second best, but rather God's best for them now; they have learned to be content in their singleness (Philippians 4:11–13). As Tim Herbert, a lifelong single person, says, 'I've now got the point of assuming it's not going to happen, but not yet to the point of hoping it won't! I guess that means that I'm comfortable with the way things are, with the way I am.'[22]

3   Another group of people may be described as *reluctantly single*, because they struggle with not being married. For many this will be because they have not yet found the right partner or maybe have been rejected in some way. This is a hard place to be in, since not getting married when you want to be married can raise many questions about both the goodness of God and one's own self-worth. Feelings of disappointment and rejection swirl around them. They may wonder why no one has chosen them or why God has not allowed them to have the very precious gift of a life-partner and the chance of having children. These are deep-seated issues that need exploring in a safe and accepting environment. The only way anyone can finally come to peace is by resting in the unconditional love of God and offering themselves in surrender to his good and perfect will – but no one is pretending that this is easy or that there is a once-for-all moment of surrender that will bring an end to their loneliness or longing.

Those who truly embrace singleness discover that this state has many benefits. Rather than being tied down, single people are free to follow God wherever he leads, to be spontaneous in the way they live, to choose to do the things they want to do. Single people who thrive generally build a good support network for themselves, are socially active and find a sense of belonging through family ties, church friendships and other close relationships. At the same time, there are drawbacks – occasionally feeling lonely and the sudden resurfacing of the longing for companionship, to have children and to be a grandparent. Occasionally it means being misunderstood by some people ('Are you gay?') and patronised by others ('When will you settle down?').

At the heart of everything is the core issue of knowing our identity in Christ (chapter 6) and of finding our needs met in him – he is truly the lover of our souls. Some single people may envy those who are married, but anyone who is married will soon tell you it is not a bed of roses. No one person can meet the love vacuum we all carry inside us. Only God can do that, and growing intimacy with him is one way of finding satisfaction for our need for love. Tim Herbert makes this point well: 'If in Christ we are pleasing to God, why are we so fixated on that one flawed, fallible human being to somehow make us happy? Surely we should be focusing instead on how to find our complete fulfilment in Christ.'[23]

The church has a big responsibility to care for its single people, making them welcome and helping them to feel involved at all levels. For single people, the call is to fix their eyes fully on Jesus and delight themselves in him, knowing that his will is good and perfect, even if not exactly what they had in mind.

## Conversation starters

1   Which of the three groups mentioned here do you most identify with: are you willingly single, contentedly single or reluctantly single?
2   What joys do you feel about being single? What difficulties do you have about being single?
3   How do you cope with some of the pressures of the single life – loneliness, regret, comparison, temptation? In particular, how are you handling the temptation to view pornographic material or engage in sexual fantasy?
4   How are you developing supportive and accountable relationships?
5   How does your spiritual life strengthen you? How are you developing intimacy with God and increasing your awareness of being loved unconditionally by God?

## Helpful reading

Sam Allberry, 7 Myths about Singleness (Gospel Coalition, 2019)
Barry Danylak, Redeeming Singleness: How the storyline of scripture affirms the single life (Crossway, 2010)
Debbie Hawker and Tim Herbert (eds), Single Mission: Thriving as a single person in cross-cultural ministry (Condeo Press, 2013)
Al Hsu, The Single Issue (IVP, 1997)
Kate Wharton, Single-Minded: Being single, whole and living life to the full (Lion Hudson, 2016)

# 13

# Marriage

**'Haven't you read,' [Jesus] replied, 'that at the beginning the Creator "made them male and female," and said, "For this reason a man will leave his father and mother and be united to his wife, and the two will become one flesh"?'**
MATTHEW 19:4–5

Even though we live in a sexually permissive society, where relationships are often shallow and temporary, there is still a longing for the depth, stability and security that marriage can provide. Human life flourishes when it is ordered according to God's design, and marriage (the commitment of man and woman to be together for life) is part of his original plan for society. Couples thrive when they are secure in each other's love, and children prosper when they have a stable home.

The biblical teaching on marriage goes back to the creation story. Although everything that God made was good, one thing was not quite right – Adam found himself alone, which God deemed not good (Genesis 2:18). So God made a helper for Adam, and Eve was given to him to be his companion, bone of his bones and flesh of his flesh (Genesis 2:23). In the security of this relationship they enjoyed not only the deepest friendship but also the closest intimacy, for they were naked and not ashamed. These benefits – an end to loneliness and the blessing of being known, loved and accepted just as we are – remain at the heart of God's intention for marriage.

Of course being created as male and female made it possible for them to be fruitful and multiply as commanded by God (Genesis 1:27–28), and the gift of being able to create human life together was meant to take place in the context of a committed relationship, the covenant of marriage (Malachi 2:14). Sex is a beautiful gift given to us by God, but it is best enjoyed within the security of marriage, hence the saying, 'Chastity before marriage and faithfulness within marriage.' It is important to say that while most couples have the joy of having children, not all are able to do so, and this can be a cause of great disappointment and pain which others need to recognise with sensitivity.[24]

Jesus affirmed the importance of marriage in his own teaching, emphasising that in marriage, and through the sexual union, the two become one flesh (Matthew 19:6). For this reason the sanctity of marriage is to be upheld. It is never easy for two independent people to come together without some turbulence, and the best of marriages experience difficulty, so the marriage relationship is one both partners must work at and seek to strengthen. Sadly, not all marriages survive, and separation or even divorce happens. While this is regrettable, and extremely painful all round, it is not the unforgiveable sin, and forgiveness and restoration are possible for those who have been through divorce.

What is important to remember is that we must choose whom we marry with great care. We will want to marry someone who shares our faith and whose faith is on a similar level to our own. Then we should look for someone with whom we would be happy to share our whole life – someone to whom we are attracted, with whom we can communicate deeply and whose friendship we value greatly. It is always worth making sure we share similar values when it comes to our goals in life and our attitude to money, having children and relationships with in-laws. And, of course, we want to be in love with that person, not in a Hollywood kind of way, but more in a 1 Corinthians 13 way. The decision to get married should not be rushed. It is worth getting to know someone very well before deciding, spending time in prayer and seeking confirmation that we are suited from those who know us well.

Living together with another person in a marriage requires much grace and over the years not a little patience and perseverance. Marriage will soon expose our innate selfishness, and life together will provide many opportunities to mature as a person as we work through the challenges that come our way. There will be plenty of opportunity to develop the sacrificial kind of love that is expressed by the Greek word *agape*. Good marriages don't just happen; they are the result of much prayer and hard work. Here are some areas to consider.

1  *Love languages*. Each person has a unique way of giving and receiving love. Gary Chapman has identified five such ways – spending time together, giving gifts, loving touch, words of encouragement and acts of

service.[25] Take time to discover how you like to give and receive love, and then find out what works for your partner.

2  *Communication*. Perhaps the most important gift we ever give to our partner is the gift of active listening, so that we truly understand what they are thinking and feeling. This is complemented by the willingness to talk and disclose our thoughts and feelings to our partner. Good communication requires plenty of time and a conducive environment.

3  *Handling conflict*. Conflict is not wrong, and we should not feel our marriage is failing if we have disagreements. It is better to bring issues into the open than allow them to fester unresolved. Generally, we will reproduce the patterns of resolving conflict that we have known growing up, which may or may not be healthy. It may be worth taking a course on conflict resolution to help in this area.[26]

4  *Expectations*. This can apply to any area of our life (for example, the use of money, how to bring up children and so on), but in particular to our thoughts about sex. It may be difficult to articulate this at first, but over-coming our shyness and articulating our needs, as well as our fears, will help us to develop greater intimacy.

5  *Time together*. Regular 'date nights' help to maintain intimacy, but simply making sure we have enough time to talk and to enjoy the ordinary plea-sures of life together is how we stay close. This becomes more important as work and family life increase the pressure on us. So many couples drift apart because they fail to nurture their relationship.

6  *Forgiveness and grace*. We will definitely make mistakes and hurt one another. We may even sin against our partner, deliberately or uncon-sciously. This is why we must be constantly willing to forgive and show grace to each other. It may not always be easy, but it is the only way to live and maintain a healthy relationship.

A marriage is like fine wine; it matures with age. Nowadays there is the tendency to give up on a relationship too quickly because things are difficult, but if we persevere through such times and perhaps seek outside help and counsel, we will discover that the joys of a mature marriage are even more rewarding than those we experienced in the honeymoon phase. To have travelled through life with another person, to have a shared history and a host of happy memories, provides the basis for a rich contentment in our later years, a wonderful reward for choosing to remain faithful to our vows.

## Conversation starters

1 How has your approach to marriage been influenced by what you saw as a child or have picked up from the media and society? How does the biblical teaching challenge your thinking?
2 What do you think is the purpose of marriage as God intended it? How will this influence and shape your marriage?
3 If you are not yet married, what will you look for in your partner? If you are married, what do you appreciate about your partner?
4 Of the six ingredients for a healthy marriage mentioned here, which are you doing well and which do you need to work on?
5 Are there any other issues about marriage that you would like to discuss?

## Helpful reading

Timothy Keller with Kathy Keller, *The Meaning of Marriage: Facing the complexities of commitment with the wisdom of God* (Dutton, 2011)
Nicky Lee and Sila Lee, *The Marriage Book* (Hodder and Stoughton, 2018)
Mike Mason, *The Mystery of Marriage: Meditations on the miracle* (Multnomah, 2005)
Rob Parsons, *The Sixty Minute Marriage: Transform your relationship in one hour* (Hodder and Stoughton, 2009)
Gary Thomas, *Sacred Marriage: What if God designed marriage to make us holy more than to make us happy?* (Zondervan, 2015)

# 14

# Talking Jesus

**We are therefore Christ's ambassadors, as though God were making his appeal through us. We implore you on Christ's behalf: be reconciled to God.**
2 CORINTHIANS 5:20

The call to bear witness to Christ is an essential part of discipleship. The first apostles were called to be with him and to go out and preach the gospel (Mark 3:14). Both the twelve and the seventy-two were sent on mission trips as part of their training (Mark 6:6–13; Luke 10:1–4). All of this was preparation for the great commission, when Jesus would send them into the world with the words 'Go and make disciples of all nations' ringing in their ears (Matthew 28:19). The Acts of the Apostles is the unfolding story of how, with great boldness and courage, they did just that, establishing churches and taking the gospel from Jerusalem to Rome.

A foundation stone in our understanding that the church is called to be a witness is given in Acts 1:8: 'But you will receive power when the Holy Spirit comes on you; and you will be my witnesses in Jerusalem, and in all Judea and Samaria, and to the ends of the earth.' Every individual is called to bear witness to the truth of the gospel message, as well as to share the story of how that message has impacted their life. Jesus did not hide the fact that this witness might well take place in a hostile environment (John 16:1–2), and Paul, who himself suffered much because of his witness, reminds his young protégé Timothy not to be ashamed of testifying about Jesus (2 Timothy 1:8).

In post-Christian Britain the church is in danger of losing its confidence when it comes to personal witness. Traditional Christian values and morals are scorned and ridiculed as outdated. Militant atheism challenges the veracity and credibility of Christian truth. God is a delusion, an idea we have outgrown. In a multicultural society, all religions are regarded as the same, and Christianity has no special place. It is easy to feel marginalised and defensive.

Stories of people being reprimanded for witnessing at work are intimidating, and the pressure from political correctness to conform to the new norms of sexual ethics and gender ideology forces people to keep silent about their faith. Media stories of the decline of Christianity can dishearten us, and the scandal of child abuse in Christian institutions robs the church of its moral integrity in society. As a result, we may be reluctant to identify ourselves as followers of Jesus lest we be ridiculed or scorned.

Yet the spiritual hunger in people's lives has never been so high, and many are more willing to listen to our message than we may think. Recent research has shown that Christians are well-liked and respected by their friends and colleagues, who are often happy to talk about spiritual matters. One in five adults believe that Jesus was God in human form, and 43% believe in the resurrection.[27] People are more open than we may think, but we must be sensitive and wise in our approach to faith-sharing. Confrontational approaches with dogmatic assertions are unlikely to go down well. The basis for our witness has to be that we live distinctively, with our lives matching our words and the love of God shining through us in our actions. We need to be authentic and real with people.

When we look at the story of Jesus and his conversation with the Samaritan woman in John 4, we can see two important principles for our witness today.

1   Jesus set off from Jerusalem and arrived at the well of Sychar just as the woman came to draw water at noon. This was a divine encounter, orchestrated by the Father, and all Jesus did was to notice his Father at work and respond accordingly. This is the principle of being *attentive to God*, and it is the first step in being an effective witness. God is at work, drawing people to himself, and he will initiate the openings we need. He will open doors of opportunity; we need simply to be attentive to his prior work, then respond in faith and obedience to what he is doing (see John 5:19). This realisation takes the pressure out of witnessing and makes it achievable for all.

2   Having taken notice of the woman, we then see how Jesus engaged with her at the point of her need. He saw her as a real person, made by and for God. He saw past her gender, her race and her reputation, to a woman desperately in need of fulfilment and of the living water which only he could give. He carefully unpacked what he wanted to say, line by line, going at her pace and working within her understanding. This is the

second principle, that of being *attentive to people*. We are to value individuals as those who are loved by God and worthy of respect, recognising that there is a God-shaped vacuum in every individual life.

The apostle Peter seems to bring these two principles together when writing to believers being persecuted for their faith. He urges them:

> Always be prepared to give an answer to everyone who asks you to give the reason for the hope that you have. But do this with gentleness and respect, keeping a clear conscience, so that those who speak maliciously against your good behaviour in Christ may be ashamed of their slander.
> 1 PETER 3:15–16

God will create the opportunities we need to talk about Jesus. Our part is to recognise the moment and, with the help of the Holy Spirit, to be bold enough to share wisely as much as is appropriate at that moment.

Prayer plays a significant part in this process, for it links us directly with the heart and mind of God. We can pray first of all that God will show us how to become more attentive in the way we live, both to the promptings of the Holy Spirit within us and to the people we meet in the course of our everyday lives. This may require us to slow down a bit and not be in such a rush to be on our way; to be open and friendly and have time for people.

Then we can pray that God will give us opportunities to share our faith, as the apostle Paul did: 'Pray for us, too, that God may open a door for our message, so that we may proclaim the mystery of Christ, for which I am in chains. Pray that I may proclaim it clearly, as I should' (Colossians 4:3–4). If you pray sincerely and consistently, don't be surprised when God answers.

Finally, we can pray for a handful of people who are close to us and whom God lays on our heart, so that they may come to faith. Each of us has a unique set of family, friends, work colleagues and neighbours. We may be the only Christian they know and the only one who can tell them about Jesus.

I have always regarded evangelism as my Achilles heel, feeling that I was below par when it came to sharing my faith. However since discovering the principles of being attentive to God and attentive to people, I have had many memorable opportunities to talk about Jesus with others in a natural and unselfconscious way. That doesn't mean I am leading people to Christ every week! It does mean that I am recognising on a regular basis God-given opportunities to speak openly and freely about the good news of Jesus and have been able to help some take a step nearer to him. This has made evangelism both achievable and exciting, even for me. And if that can happen for me, it can certainly happen for you as well.

## Conversation starters

1   How do you feel about evangelism? Why do you think so many Christians are hesitant to share their faith?
2   From your perspective, what are the factors in society that work against Christian witness? What needs do you see in people that can be met by the gospel?
3   What do you understand by being 'attentive to God'? How can you increase your awareness of what God is doing in the people around you?
4   How can you become more attentive to people?
5   Share any occasion when you felt God had opened the door for you to share your story and speak about Jesus.

## Helpful reading

Lewie Clark, *Imitating Jesus: Love, friendship, and disciple-making* (West Bow Press, 2012)

Michael Frost, *Surprise the World: The five habits of highly missional people* (NavPress, 2016)

J. John, *The Natural Evangelism Course* (Philo Trust, 2014)

David Male and Paul Weston, *The Word's Out: Principles and strategies for effective evangelism today*, second edition (BRF, 2019)

Rebecca Manley Pippert, *Out of the Saltshaker and into the World: Evangelism as a way of life* (IVP, 2010)

Rico Tice, *Honest Evangelism: How to talk about Jesus even when it's tough* (The Good Book Company, 2015)

Details of the Talking Jesus course can be found at **hopetogether.org.uk**

# 15

# Issues of justice

**Here is my servant, whom I uphold, my chosen one in whom I delight;
I will put my Spirit on him, and he will bring justice to the nations.**
ISAIAH 42:1

The letter of James is direct and to the point when it says, 'Faith by itself, if it is not accompanied by action, is dead' (James 2:17). It is not enough simply to say we believe in God; our faith has to be demonstrated by the way we live through our values, our behaviour and our actions. If people are in need of clothes or daily food, we cannot simply wish them well or pray that God will provide for them. We have to do something practically to help them; otherwise our faith is in vain.

This emphasis on caring for others is at the heart of biblical Christianity, rooted in the character of God himself, who is a just God. Moses joyfully proclaimed, 'He is the Rock, his works are perfect, and all his ways are just. A faithful God who does no wrong, upright and just is he' (Deuteronomy 32:4). Prophets like Micah carefully articulated the heart of true religion: 'He has shown you, O mortal, what is good. And what does the Lord require of you? To act justly and to love mercy and to walk humbly with your God' (Micah 6:8). When the people of Israel forgot this basic responsibility, the prophets quickly reminded them of God's displeasure: 'Take your evil deeds out of my sight; stop doing wrong. Learn to do right; seek justice. Defend the oppressed. Take up the cause of the fatherless; plead the case of the widow' (Isaiah 1:16–17).

We are familiar with the idea of a manifesto from the political arena. The manifesto of Jesus was focused on bringing God's justice to the world. At the start of his ministry he laid out his vision, using the words of Isaiah 61:1–2. He declared:

The Spirit of the Lord is on me,
>because he has anointed me
>to proclaim good news to the poor.
He has sent me to proclaim freedom for the prisoners
>and recovery of sight for the blind,
to set the oppressed free,
>to proclaim the year of the Lord's favour.
LUKE 4:18–19

He taught his followers that when they involved themselves in serving others, they were in fact serving him: 'For I was hungry and you gave me something to eat, I was thirsty and you gave me something to drink, I was a stranger and you invited me in, I needed clothes and you clothed me, I was ill and you looked after me, I was in prison and you came to visit me' (Matthew 25:35–36). It was this truth that moved and motivated Mother Teresa to work among the poor in Kolkata with her Sisters of Mercy. As she helped the destitute and dying, she believed she was helping Christ himself.

The Jerusalem church quickly organised themselves to meet the needs around them, daily distributing food to widows and others and appointing key leaders to the task to see that it was done fairly and well (Acts 6:1–6). Individuals like Dorcas expressed their discipleship by doing good and helping the poor, in her case making garments for them to wear (Acts 9:36–39). The apostle Paul taught that anyone who did not provide for their relatives and household was denying the faith and was worse than an unbeliever (1 Timothy 5:8).

Reflecting on the range of biblical material Matthew Knell sums up its teaching like this:

> Seeing that God is just, that His people are called to be just, and that Jesus embodies the justice of God, the church is then called to reflect Jesus and be agents realising the will of God on earth – including the establishment of justice – as it is done in heaven.[28]

Church history shows that when God's people have been passionate about their faith, they have always involved themselves in social justice. Think, for example, of William Wilberforce (1759–1833) and the abolition of slavery or William Booth (1829–1912) and the work of the Salvation Army among the poor of inner-city London. Not all Christians, however, welcomed the emphasis on social action, fearing that busy activity would take precedence over preaching the gospel. Evangelicals in particular were wary of drifting away from this biblical essential until the Lausanne Congress of 1974. There the great Christian statesman John Stott convinced delegates that there should be a synthesis between evangelism and social action. 'If we truly love our neighbour we shall without doubt tell him the Good News of Jesus,' he said. 'But equally if we truly love our neighbour we won't stop there… Love… expresses itself in service wherever it sees need.'[29]

Since that watershed moment there has been a plethora of God-directed initiatives aimed at correcting the injustices and imbalances of society and bringing relief and hope to the marginalised and vulnerable. At last we are learning that proclamation and demonstration go together, that grace should make us just. Think of some of these organisations with a Christian foundation – Christians Against Poverty (CAP), The Trussell Trust's food banks, Operation Mobilisation's mercy ships and the interdenominational network of Street Pastors in many town centres. Or consider what these (and other) mission agencies are doing in different parts of the world – Tearfund, World Vision, Open Doors and Mission Aviation Fellowship, to name just a few.

Today you will find Christians actively involving themselves in chaplaincy to sports clubs, schools, hospitals, police and fire services. Others are working tirelessly combating knife crime, modern-day slavery, homelessness, drug addiction and sex trafficking. Local churches are doing their part, too, with toddler groups, drop-in clubs, lunch clubs, youth programmes and welcoming asylum seekers and refugees. More recently Christians have at last begun to see that we have a responsibility to care for creation, to be responsible consumers and to care for the environment. We are waking up, too, to the importance of racial equality and making sure that people are accepted for who they are and not judged by the colour of their skin.

Yet all of us know how difficult it can be to lift ourselves out of our spiritual complacency or to break free from the shackles of our comfortable lifestyles. Sometimes we just don't see the need or have not yet caught the vision of God's call to walk justly. Perhaps we need to read our Bibles again and understand God's agenda for our world so that we can join him in his good purposes for all people.

Just Love is a fairly new organisation in the UK with a vision to inspire and release Christian students to pursue the biblical call to social justice.

They want to make a difference through their careers, giving, lifestyle and communities. 'What if every Christian student shared our passion for social justice and did something about it?' asks one of the founders, Tom Christmas. 'What would it say to our university if all Christians were known for their radical, sacrificial love for those on the margins? What sort of a difference would it make to our city if hundreds of Christian students started volunteering, fundraising, campaigning, praying?'[30]

That rallying cry is not just for students but for all who take discipleship seriously and have a passion for Jesus and, as a result, a passion for justice. How can we begin? Here are some simple first steps:

1  Pray for those involved in engagement with the needs of society and for God to direct you as to how to be involved. Ask for a specific area of need to focus on.
2  Join in any activities or programmes your local church may have.
3  Support organisations working on the front line, financially and in prayer.
4  Try volunteering in a project locally.
5  Campaign and advocate along with others for justice and transformation.

When the needs of society continue to increase, the church cannot be silent or inactive. We must let our voice be heard and give our time and resources to making a difference.

## Conversation starters

1  Why is theology the basis for social action? How does the nature of God move us to get involved in caring for people and creation?
2  What scriptures stand out for you as giving a call to justice?
3  What examples have you seen personally where people have lived out their faith in practical, down-to-earth ways? How do these speak to you?
4  What do you consider are some of the reasons why churches have generally been slow to engage with the social needs in their communities? How can this reticence be overcome?
5  What do you think God is saying to you as you ponder all of this? What first step might you take?

## Helpful reading

Jason Fileta (ed.), *Live Justly* (Micah Challenge, 2014)

Gary Haugen, *Good News about Injustice: A witness of courage in a hurting world*, tenth anniversary edition (IVP, 2009)

Martin J. Hodson and Margot R. Hodson, *A Christian Guide to Environmental Issues* (BRF, 2015)

Timothy Keller, *Generous Justice: How God's grace makes us just* (Hodder and Stoughton, 2010)

Richard Stearns, *The Hole in Our Gospel* (Thomas Nelson, 2009)

'Live Justly', a six-part course available from Micah Challenge at **livejust.ly**

# Going deeper

# 16

# Spiritual disciplines

**They devoted themselves to the apostles' teaching and to fellowship, to the breaking of bread and to prayer.**
ACTS 2:42

Growth in the Christian does not happen by chance, and it is not automatic. Neither is it all down to God, although he is always the initiator. We have our part to play, and in order to cooperate with the work of God within us we must build into our lives the kind of practices that will foster the growth we desire. Such practices are called spiritual disciplines or holy habits – the things we do to prepare ourselves to receive God's transforming grace.

We practise such disciplines not to gain merit before God but because we want to respond to God's initiative in our lives. The disciplines make it easier for us to access the life of God and receive more of his grace. Richard Foster, one of the foremost writers on the disciplines, states:

> A farmer is helpless to grow grain; all he can do is to provide the right conditions for the growing of grain. He puts the seed in the ground where the natural forces take over and up comes the grain. That is the way with the Spiritual Disciplines – they are a way of sowing to the Spirit.[31]

In the Jerusalem church described in the book of Acts, the disciples quickly learned that, although they had received the Spirit at Pentecost, they still had a part to play in developing their relationship with God. Luke describes four basic disciplines they followed, which, as simple as they are, formed the foundation for the vibrant spirituality seen in the early church (Acts 2:42):

1  Disciples are those who learn, so we find that they gave themselves to learning about their faith (*the apostles' teaching*).

2   Growth never takes place in isolation but in the company of other believers, so sharing life with one another was a priority (*fellowship*).
3   Worship was central to their way of life, in particular remembering Jesus and his death in the way he had instructed them to (*the breaking of bread*).
4   Aware of their dependency on God, they regularly sought God's blessing on their lives and for him to be at work in their midst (*prayer*).

No believer can expect to develop spiritually if these four basic practices are ignored, but when they become integrated into our lives they form the basis for a healthy, Spirit-filled life of discipleship. Notice the word 'devoted' in this context – these were habits of life that they practised in a disciplined way, but out of love, not duty. This is the essence of the devotional life.

In his book *Holy Habits*, Methodist minister Andrew Roberts studies Acts 2:42–47 in depth. To the four practices already mentioned he identifies six more that seem to have been integral to life in the church from its inception:

- sharing resources (v. 44)
- serving (v. 45)
- eating together (v. 46)
- gladness and generosity (v. 46)
- worship (v. 47)
- making more disciples (v. 47).

These practices he describes as 'composite parts of a habitual holy way of living' both for individuals and churches, and it is his conviction that congregations who adopt it as a way of life today will experience spiritual renewal.[32]

While Roberts has identified ten basic disciplines, this by no means exhausts the ways by which we may deepen our walk with God. Other writers, like Richard Foster and Dallas Willard, have compiled their own lists, but none of them would claim that such compilations are anything more than *possible* ways of engaging with God. We must avoid being legalistic ('this is what you must do') and prescriptive ('this is the right way to do it') when it comes to the disciplines. They are many and varied to suit individual needs and personalities. Different practices may be helpful in different seasons of our lives. We should not be afraid to ring the changes so that our devotional life remains fresh and relevant.

What is important is that we develop a regular pattern, or rule of life, to help us abide in Christ. Pete Greig, founder of the 24–7 prayer movement, defines a rule of life as 'a set of principles and practices we build into the rhythm of our daily lives, helping us to deepen our relationship with God and to serve him more faithfully'.[33]

With that in mind, and with the Acts 2:42 disciplines as a foundation, my own spiritual practice revolves around six particular disciplines, which you may find helpful too.

First, the three disciplines that bring us closer to God:

1  *Stillness*, the habit of slowing down and resting in order to focus for a while on our relationship with God. Life is so often lived at a pace and filled with hurry and haste, leaving little time or room for God, but the Lord says, 'Be still, and know that I am God' (Psalm 46:10).

2  *Silence*, the habit of switching off from the noisy world in which we live in order to hear God's voice, in particular the still, small voice within us. As Elijah discovered, God is often heard not in the wind, earthquake or fire, but in a gentle whisper (1 Kings 19:11–13). Silence is essential to hearing God speak.

3  *Solitude*, the habit of withdrawing from the demands of life for a time in order to be alone with God and give our time and attention to him alone. This was a practice often seen in the life of Jesus (Luke 5:15–16) and which he taught his disciples (Mark 6:30–31). Yes, we need to be in fellowship with others, but we also need periods when we are by ourselves.

Then the three disciplines that take us deeper into God:

4  *Reflection*, the habit of taking time to think and to consider one's life before God. Sometimes we are so busy living our life that we have no idea where it is going. Reflection helps us to stay on course, and honest self-examination opens us up to areas in our life that may need to change (2 Corinthians 13:5).

5 *Bible meditation*, the habit of pondering the meaning of scripture so that we internalise its message in such a way that not only do we believe it, but we also live by it. Meditation, or prayerful reflection upon God's word, helps the truth of God sink from our heads into our hearts, to be acted on by our will (Psalm 1:1–3).

6 *Contemplation*, the discipline of giving our loving attention to the one who is the lover of our souls, of taking time to rest in God's presence and allow ourselves to relax in his boundless love (Psalm 27:4).

I find that these six disciplines work particularly well together, especially in the context of a personal retreat – a period of a few days set aside to be alone with God and to seek his presence more intentionally. Such times have been especially transformative for me personally and are part of my own rule of life.

Keeping sabbath would also be for many a very precious discipline. By sabbath we mean weekly time set aside from normal working life in order to worship and have fellowship with others, but also to relax, have time for rest and do things that help us to be refreshed. For some this may coincide with Sunday, but for others it may be another day in the week. This is a discipline given to us by God for our well-being and not only established at creation, when God rested (Genesis 2:2–3), but also included in the ten commandments (Exodus 20:8–11), further emphasising its importance. See chapter 24.

Spiritual disciplines don't by themselves transform us, but they bring us more consciously into the realm of God's love, where change can take place. While grace is opposed to earning (we do not have to merit God's help), it is not opposed to effort (we do have a part to play in working out our salvation). The disciplines help us to cooperate with God in this process of change. They are to be used in a context of grace, not law; of secrecy, not display. We will need the help of the Holy Spirit to establish our own pattern of devotion. It is not a matter of trying harder or doing more, but of asking God to give us a hunger to know him more and then responding to his invitations. Remember too that these are personal disciplines and will work best when they reflect our individuality and uniqueness.

## Conversation starters

1 What spiritual practices make up your devotional life? Are you satisfied that you are intentional enough in seeking God?
2 What do you think about the idea of a rule of life? What might this look like for you?
3 What is your response to the three disciplines that bring us closer to God?
4 What is your response to the three disciplines that take us deeper into God?
5 How do you currently keep sabbath? What are your thoughts about retreat?

## Helpful reading

Adele Ahlberg Calhoun, *Spiritual Disciplines Handbook: Practices that transform us* (IVP, 2005)
Richard Foster, *Celebration of Discipline: The path to spiritual growth* (Hodder and Stoughton, 1980)
Tony Horsfall, *Rhythms of Grace: Finding intimacy with God in a busy life* (BRF, 2012)
Andrew Roberts, *Holy Habits* (Malcolm Down, 2016)
Dallas Willard, *Spirit of the Disciplines: Understanding how God changes lives* (Hodder and Stoughton, 1998)

# 17

# Personal transformation

**And we all, who with unveiled faces contemplate the Lord's glory, are being transformed into his image with ever-increasing glory, which comes from the Lord, who is the Spirit.**
2 CORINTHIANS 3:18

As we seek to grow into maturity as followers of Christ, we must give attention to the development of our character. In a culture where great emphasis is placed on gifting, and character matters very little, we find that the opposite is true in the kingdom of God. For disciples, character comes first and gifting second. Indeed, we can say that a sound character forms the foundation for the exercise of our gifting. Without solid character we may easily shipwreck any ministry we have by inappropriate behaviours or temperamental flaws.

God's priority is to make us like his Son, and this is the purpose for which he called us in the first place: 'God knew what he was doing from the very beginning. He decided from the outset to shape the lives of those who love him along the same lines as the life of his Son' (Romans 8:29, MSG). This transformation is something he does, but it involves a process with which we cooperate, and not just passively but actively – welcoming the changes he wants to bring to our lives and intentionally seeking character growth. The character of Christ is best understood in terms of the fruit of the Spirit: love, joy, peace, forbearance, kindness, goodness, faithfulness, gentleness and self-control (Galatians 5:22–23). When these qualities are consistently seen in us, we are becoming like Christ. But how does it happen?

I believe there are six aspects to this inner transformation, like the six points of the Star of David. Think of this star as one triangle inverted and placed on top of another. The first triangle represents what God does as he works in us; the second triangle is what we do as we cooperate with the process of transformation.

What does God do?

1 He works in us by the *Holy Spirit*, who is the agent of change. Negatively, the Spirit convicts us, showing us where we are not like Christ and reminding us where we need to change. This disillusionment with the way we are is the precursor to any real change. We must want to change, like Isaiah in the temple: '"Woe to me!" I cried. "I am ruined! For I am a man of unclean lips, and I live among a people of unclean lips, and my eyes have seen the King, the Lord Almighty"' (Isaiah 6:5). Positively, the Spirit empowers us, not leaving us in our despair but responding to our cry for help by forming the life of Christ within us so that we can change. Christlikeness is the fruit of the Spirit's work within us. He gives us both the desire to want to be like Jesus and the power to break free from unhelpful patterns of behaviour.

2 He speaks to us through *the scriptures*, which provide the pattern for change, showing us a new way of living and giving us an understanding of his will for our lives. Through the gospels we can see what Jesus was like, and through the epistles in particular we learn that he lives within us. Again, scripture shows us where we may be wrong but also points us in the direction of what is right: 'All Scripture is God-breathed and is useful for teaching, rebuking, correcting and training in righteousness, so that the servant of God may be thoroughly equipped for every good work' (2 Timothy 3:16–17). We must place ourselves under the scrutiny and discipline of scripture, and be willing to make any necessary adjustments, if our lives are to come into line with that of Christ.

3 He orchestrates the *circumstances* of our lives so that we are humbled of our pride and learn to depend on him. Through trials and difficulty he shapes our character and bends our will. This is the context of change, and God is always at work in the events of our lives to shape our character. Joseph suffered much at the hands of his brothers and was taken as a slave to Egypt. God used his many adversities to prepare him for the responsibility that lay ahead when he would be given prominence in Egypt and the opportunity to save his people. With hindsight he could say to his brothers, 'So then, it was not you who sent me here, but God' (Genesis 45:8). They had intended to harm him, but God used it for good, to change him and to put him in a place where he could help his family (Genesis 50:20; Romans 8:28).

What do we do?

1   We practise the *spiritual disciplines*, by which we place ourselves in the
    way of grace. We study the Bible, spend time in prayer, take part in Chris-
    tian community, worship regularly, practise giving, serve other people
    and so on, all as a way of drawing closer to God and expressing our faith.
    These provide the means of change. Disciplines like these (or holy habits,
    as they are called – see chapter 16) are not an end in themselves and
    should never be practised rigidly to gain God's favour. They are channels
    by which the grace of God can be communicated to us and simply help
    us to prepare ourselves to receive that grace. Thus we read that in the
    early days of the Jerusalem church, the believers 'devoted themselves
    to the apostles' teaching and to fellowship, to the breaking of bread and
    to prayer' (Acts 2:42).

2   We spend time alone in *personal reflection*, examining our lives before
    God, listening to his voice and receiving his love into our hearts. We seek
    to know ourselves as people and to understand who we are in Christ. This
    is the method of change. It is interesting that the apostle Paul, after his
    conversion and initial entry into ministry, withdrew for a time to Arabia,
    where he spent time alone seeking God. We know very little about these
    hidden years, except that God must have used them to deepen the work of
    grace in his life and, in his own words, 'to reveal his Son in me' (Galatians
    1:15–17). We may not be able to put so much time aside for reflection,
    but incorporating the discipline of retreat into our lives occasionally will
    pay rich dividends for any who truly desire transformation.

3   We meet with *others who are passionate for God*, soul friends with whom
    we share our faith journey, and perhaps a mentor or spiritual director to
    advise us. We are open and vulnerable, allowing these trusted friends to
    give us feedback and help us become more self-aware. Their example
    inspires us to be the best that we can be. Here we find the motivation
    for change. Full transformation seldom happens in isolation, since we
    are made for community. We need to be in relationship with God and
    others, to be stimulated, comforted and challenged. That's why intention-
    ally meeting together with others for the purpose of spiritual growth is
    essential: 'And let us consider how we may spur one another on towards
    love and good deeds, not giving up meeting together, as some are in the
    habit of doing, but encouraging one another – and all the more as you
    see the Day approaching' (Hebrews 10:24–25).

Such transformation is a lifelong process, of course, and most of us have days when we feel we are doing well and other days when we despair at our lack of progress! But on the whole, if we give ourselves to the process, change will be taking place. We may not always be aware of what is happening, because true goodness is always unselfconscious, but others will be able to see the difference that God is making in our lives. It is the people closest to us who will be best placed to assess our progress in Christlikeness.

## Conversation starters

1  How do you understand the connection between character and gifting in the Christian life?
2  Can you describe one aspect of your character that has changed for the better since you became a believer?
3  Consider the part that God plays in our transformation – how have you seen God at work in your life?
4  Consider the part that we play in our transformation – what are you presently doing to aid the process of change?
5  Which area of your character would you most like to see change as you journey into Christlikeness?

## Helpful reading

Tim Chester, *You Can Change: God's transforming power for our sinful behavior and negative emotions* (IVP, 2008)
Pamela Evans, *Shaping the Heart: Reflections on spiritual formation and fruitfulness* (BRF, 2011)
James Bryan Smith, *The Good and Beautiful Life: Putting on the character of Christ* (IVP, 2009)
Stephen W. Smith, *Soul Shaping: A practical guide for spiritual transformation* (David C. Cook, 2011)
Dallas Willard, *Renovation of the Heart: Putting on the character of Christ* (NavPress, 2002)

# 18

# Growing in self-knowledge

**Search me, God, and know my heart; test me and know my anxious thoughts. Se if there is any offensive way in me, and lead me in the way everlasting.**
PSALM 139:23–24

John Calvin begins his famous *Institutes of the Christian Religion* with the assertion that the knowledge of God and the knowledge of self are insepara-bly bound together. We cannot know God without knowing ourselves, and the more we truly know ourselves the more we will know God. What he means, I think, is that if we come to know ourselves properly, we will instinctively feel our deep need of God; and as we get to know God more and feel the contrast between himself (holy) and ourselves (sinful), we will come to appreciate more and more his love and grace towards us. It is in this context of knowing and being known that deep-seated transformation can take place.

Psalm 139 is the most personal of all David's psalms, describing his aware-ness that he is known by God, the God who made him and formed him in his mother's womb. Nothing is hidden from this all-seeing God, and there is no hiding place from his searching gaze: 'You have searched me, Lord, and you know me,' he says (v. 1). His behaviour, movements and motivations are all exposed, yet being completely known by God like this is not disturbing to him. Rather it is reassuring, for he knows himself to be loved and accepted by God as he is, with no need for pretence: 'How precious to me are your thoughts, God,' he says (v. 17).

Alongside this we must place Psalm 51, which details his restoration to God after his sin with Bathsheba. It is a brutally honest account of his inner dialogue with God as he comes to terms with his own sinfulness and the mercy of God towards him. His failure has awoken him to the reality of his own sinful tendencies, yet because he knows God to be merciful and gracious, the possibility of forgiveness and restored joy is real. 'Have mercy on me, O God, according to your unfailing love,' he cries. 'According to your great compassion blot out my transgressions,' he pleads (v. 1). He stands before God naked and ashamed (knowing himself) but with the hope of restoration and renewal (knowing God).

David's testimony highlights for us the fact that both knowing God and knowing ourselves are foundational to spiritual growth and maturity. Psychologist David Benner says, 'Deep knowing of God and deep knowing of self always develop interactively. The result is the authentic transformation of the self that is at the core of Christian spirituality.'[34] In this chapter we focus on growing in our self-knowledge, something that is not easy, because it can be painful and we are all masters of deceiving ourselves – and sometimes others – into thinking we are better than we really are.

The self-knowledge we seek has two component parts: self-awareness and self-understanding.

1 *Self-awareness* is the understanding of how we relate to other people and how our behaviour affects them. How do we impact other people? How do they experience us? Without such awareness we may well develop certain blind spots. For instance, we may not realise that we dominate conversations, are too loud and intimidate others. If such behaviour is never pointed out to us, we will continue to do these things and over time this behaviour will be reinforced, making it even more difficult to change. Not only that, but it may undermine the work we do and our effectiveness as disciples. We may remain completely oblivious to what others see as an obvious character flaw.

2 *Self-understanding* is more to do with knowing how we respond in certain situations that may trigger unhelpful behaviour in us. It is about knowing what our strong points are as well as being aware of our weaknesses. If we understand ourselves well, we can manage our behaviour and responses; if we don't, we are vulnerable to behaving less well and again under-mining our other good work. For example, if we are prone to comparing ourselves to other people, we may feel jealous of their success. If we have a great need for affirmation, we may become people-pleasers who can never say 'No' to others and are therefore constantly overwhelmed with too much to do. Understanding what makes us 'tick' is a vital factor in our journey to maturity.

But how do we come to such self-knowledge?

1  When we read *scripture*, we are constantly being confronted by ourselves as we explore the stories of the men and women of old who followed God. We see in their lives something of our own, and if we are wise we learn from their mistakes without repeating them and follow their example of faith by imitating them. At the same time the principles and teaching of the Bible guide our behaviour and help shape our characters as we apply them to our lives. In this way we have a mirror by which we can see ourselves. James puts it like this:

> Anyone who listens to the word but does not do what it says is like someone who looks at his face in a mirror and, after looking at himself, goes away and immediately forgets what he looks like. But whoever looks intently into the perfect law that gives freedom and continues in it – not forgetting what they have heard but doing it – they will be blessed in what they do.
> JAMES 1:23–25

2  *Self-reflection* is another avenue by which we gain self-knowledge. I do not mean by this a morbid introspection filled with negativity, but a healthy ability to evaluate one's own life. It was Socrates who said that the unexamined life is not worth living. Take time to think carefully about the things that happen to you, both good and bad. What can you learn from such events? If something went well, what was the reason? If something didn't go well, why was that – what might you avoid another time? Evaluating our lives in this way takes time and is best done in the context of stillness and silence, such as in a retreat setting or by taking a morning to be quiet and reflective.

3  *Journaling* is a great way to reflect. It is different from keeping a diary. In journaling, you write down your thoughts and feelings about your life and the situations you are facing. It is a way of processing in words, of thinking aloud by writing things down as honestly as possible. It is not about good grammar or perfect spelling but about expressing yourself in a way that helps you make sense of your life. Those who journal regularly like to review what they have written every so often to see if common themes emerge. Journaling can be whatever you make it. Some like to doodle and colour, others to make a scrapbook. Be as creative as you want to be, but remember the purpose: to learn about yourself in relation to God.

4  *Friends and trusted advisors* are another source of self-knowledge. Having the confidence to open ourselves up to others takes courage, but it pays rich dividends. Others can often see what we can't see ourselves. They can affirm us and challenge us, recognise our potential and spot our weaknesses. Of course, we cannot do this with everyone. We can only entrust ourselves to those who are wise, gracious and non-judgemental, but who are also willing to be honest with us. Such friendships and connections are like gold. It's why mentoring relationships are so special.

5  I have been helped greatly by learning from *psychometric tests and other tools* that give us insight into our personality and gifting. One of the most popular is the Myers-Briggs Personality Type Indicator (MBTI), which is a proven way of understanding ourselves and others. Using four different scales it helps us understand whether we are introverts or extroverts; detailed or big-picture people; those who make decisions based on logic or relationships; and organised and planned or free-flowing and spontaneous. It has immediate relevance not only to how we live our own life, but also to how we relate to others, particularly in relationships or in work teams. It also provides valuable insights into how we relate to God.[35]

The book of Proverbs urges us to turn our ear to wisdom and apply our hearts to understanding – 'Indeed, if you call out for insight and cry aloud for understanding, and if you look for it as for silver and search for it as for hidden treasure, then you will understand the fear of the Lord and find the knowledge of God' (2:3–5). Self-knowledge will bring its own reward in terms of enhancing the process of transformation that is happening in our lives.

## Conversation starters

1  How do you think knowing God and knowing one's self are linked?
2  Can you give an example of your self-awareness?
3  Can you give an example of your self-understanding?
4  What steps are you taking to grow in self-knowledge? Which of the suggestions here may help you?
5  How do we distinguish introspection from healthy self-examination?

## Helpful reading

David G. Benner, *The Gift of Being Yourself: The sacred call to self-discovery*, expanded edition (IVP, 2015)

Alan Jamieson, *Chrysalis: The hidden transformation in the journey of faith* (Paternoster, 2007)

Sybil MacBeth, *Praying in Colour: Drawing a new path to God* (Paraclete Press, 2007)

Sheila Julian Merryweather, *Colourful Prayer: A new way to pray when words are inadequate* (Kevin Mayhew, 2003)

Pete Scazzero, *Emotionally Healthy Spirituality: Unleash a revolution in your life in Christ* (Thomas Nelson, 2006)

# 19

# Facing temptation

**When tempted, no one should say, 'God is tempting me.' For God cannot be tempted by evil, nor does he tempt anyone; but each person is tempted when they are dragged away by their own evil desire and enticed.**
JAMES 1:13–14

In his book *Money, Sex and Power*, Richard Foster wrote about what I regard as Satan's three main avenues of attack on God's people. None of these is wrong in themselves, but historically they have formed the battleground of personal holiness. 'The crying need today,' he wrote, 'is for people of faith to live faithfully. This is true in all spheres of human existence, but it is particularly true with reference to money, sex and power.'[36] Speaking metaphorically, Foster describes the 'demon' that lurks beside each one of these powerful forces: the demon in money is greed; the demon in sex is lust; and the demon in power is pride.

## Money

The Bible (and Jesus in particular) has a lot to say about money, most notably that 'you cannot serve God and mammon [the spiritual power behind materialism]' (Matthew 6:24, RSV) and that 'the love of money is a root of all kinds of evil' (1 Timothy 6:10). Greed seems to be at the heart of so much of the world's economic woes, while serious gambling has become a leisure activity encouraged in so many societies despite its dangers.

Assuming we have avoided the obvious traps of stealing and dealing dishonestly, it is always helpful to consider the place that money has in our lives, how we use it and how it influences our behaviour and decision-making. We may discover that we are more materialistic than we thought, are less generous than we would like to be and gain far too much of our security from our own accumulation of wealth. Even the lack of money can bring a snare, leading us away from contentment and into an unhelpful anxiety or resentful griping.

## Sex

Scripture is very positive in its approach to sex, seeing it as one of God's good gifts to us to be exercised responsibly and joyfully within the context of marriage. In the west, almost all the accepted standards of Christian morality have been overturned nowadays, and many Christians are in a dilemma about how they should express their sexuality. Consequently the temptation to immorality is stronger than ever because ungodly behaviour seems so normal. It is the virgin who is abnormal, the faithful spouse who is naive. Experimentation is recommended and freedom of expression encouraged. In such a context Christians must establish clear boundaries in all their relationships, be aware when they are vulnerable and, like Joseph, know how to 'flee' when temptation beckons (1 Corinthians 6:18). A moment's pleasure can cost a hard-won reputation; a foolish choice can destroy a lifetime's work.

Nor is the danger only in what is done. These days, because of internet access, the potential impact on our thought life is greater than ever. The rise of the pornography industry is staggering, and the easy availability of hardcore porn is alarming. Those who feel lonely or have unmet intimacy needs are particularly vulnerable to this secret and hidden danger. Because it doesn't appear to directly affect other people, it can be justified as harmless fun, but of course it is degrading both to those who take part and those who watch. It may also be crippling to future intimacy in marriage.

## Power

The dangers of power are constantly seen in politics and secular organis-ations, but churches and Christian organisations are not immune from the misuse of authority. What is so dangerous about it is that abusive power can masquerade as 'real' leadership, that which is forthright and clear, bold and visionary. Our models of leadership may be based so much on those in society that we do not see the danger of using Christian leadership as a vehicle for our own drive for success and need to make a mark. The potential for pride that lurks within the exercise of all power and authority can make us blind to the way we treat others and deal with them. It takes a humble person to handle power well.

Power is at the heart of leadership, and those in leadership must be aware of its corrupting effect. Whatever power or authority we have over others must be handled carefully and must have a strong ethical basis to it – for example, the conviction that the best use of power is to empower others. Power should never be used to belittle others, to bully them or to take advantage of them in any way. It requires us to constantly remind ourselves that we have been entrusted with the influence that power brings and that we are answerable to God for the way we use it.

From his work talking with and listening to church leaders, Keith Farmer notes a pattern that increases their vulnerability:

> In general, the process is as follows: the stresses of leadership – such as criticism, people leaving the church, and lack of effective bound-aries – lead to very negative self-talk. For example, the leader may say to themselves, 'I am a failure as a leader.' This in turn leads to compen-satory behaviour of a self-indulgent and/or addictive nature. Examples are pornography, gluttony, and overconsumption of alcohol.[37]

What is true of church leaders is also true of others. When we are most stressed, we are also most vulnerable to temptation.

The temptations behind money, sex and power are interrelated and affect us all – young and old, male and female. They are found in Christian settings as much as elsewhere – in any congregation on a Sunday morning, in any small group that meets midweek, among ministers and missionaries, in youth groups, among deacons, and in any church leadership team. Times of lone-liness, tiredness and pressure make us all more susceptible to temptation.

How does God keep us when we are facing temptation? The apostle Paul supplies part of the answer:

So, if you think you are standing firm, be careful that you don't fall! No temptation has overtaken you except what is common to mankind. And God is faithful; he will not let you be tempted beyond what you can bear. But when you are tempted, he will also provide a way out so that you can endure it.

1 CORINTHIANS 10:12–13

We can see here five steps to overcoming temptation:

1 Stay humble and remember that without God's help you are vulnerable.
2 Don't blame yourself for feeling the pull of temptation; it is part of our common humanity and God is aware of your weakness.
3 Believe that God will be faithful to you, that he knows the limit you can bear and that he will not allow you to be tempted beyond it. You are able to resist, and you do have the strength to do so, however weak you may feel or however strong the temptation.
4 Look for the way of escape that is always there – saying 'No', avoiding a compromising situation, being accountable to a close friend, not exposing yourself to danger and so on.
5 Expect to be victorious, and when you have come through, give the glory to God.

This is not to say that it will be easy. Many of us will fight a real battle with temptation, and it will take every fibre of our spiritual muscle to overcome, but it can be done. If we do fail, we must remember that forgiveness is readily available to us as long as we are willing to confess our sin and turn away from it. Sometimes we will be able to work this out for ourselves before God; at other times we may need the help of a counsellor, mentor or friend (John 20:23; Galatians 6:1).

## Conversation starters

1 What temptations have you faced when it comes to money?
2 What temptations do you face when it comes to sex?
3 How might you be tempted to misuse or abuse power?
4 What can help us resist temptation? What do you do when you feel vulnerable?
5 To whom would you turn if you need help in finding forgiveness?

## Helpful reading

Richard Foster, *Money, Sex and Power: The challenge of the disciplined life* (Hodder and Stoughton, 1985)

Craig Gross with Jason Harper, *Eyes of Integrity: The porn pandemic and how it affects you* (Baker Books, 2010)

Claire Musters, *Taking off the Mask: Daring to be the person God created you to be* (Authentic, 2017)

Mandy Smith, *The Vulnerable Pastor: How human limitations empower our ministry* (IVP, 2015)

Shellie R. Warren, *Pure Heart: A woman's guide to sexual integrity* (Baker Books, 2010)

# 20

# Tested through trials

**Dear friends, do not be surprised at the fiery ordeal that has come on you to test you, as though something strange were happening to you.**
1 PETER 4:12

A common threat to our perseverance as disciples comes in the form of trials, the challenging events that life throws at us which have the potential to destabilise our faith and make us want to give up. We should not be surprised that we are exposed to the hardships of life in a fallen world in the same way that others are. The apostle Paul warned his new converts, 'We must go through many hardships to enter the kingdom of God' (Acts 14:22). He himself experienced a painful 'thorn in the flesh' and suffered a whole catalogue of traumatic events, including beatings, imprisonment, shipwreck, hunger and thirst, sleepless nights, homelessness and his life often being in danger. Additionally he had the stress of looking after the churches in his care (see 2 Corinthians 11:23–29; 12:7–10).

The clearest understanding of the nature and purpose of trials is given to us by James, the brother of Jesus. He writes:

> Consider it pure joy, my brothers and sisters, whenever you face trials of many kinds, because you know that the testing of your faith produces perseverance. Let perseverance finish its work so that you may be mature and complete, not lacking anything.
> JAMES 1:2–4

Trials come in many shapes and sizes and take many different forms. For example, they might be:

- *Practical* – things breaking down, shortages of money, lack of resources, plans not working out.

- *Physical* – sickness and health issues, tiredness, accidents, opposition, persecution.
- *Emotional* – relationship difficulties, dealing with conflict, worries about family, feelings of inadequacy, stress.
- *Spiritual* – oppression from the enemy, difficulties in prayer, feeling far from God, lack of visible results.
- *Mental* – worry and anxiety, difficulty making decisions and problem solving, falling into a negative mindset.

What all these trials do is to challenge our faith, forcing us to ask searching questions like: 'Is God really with me? Am I doing the right thing? Can I cope with this?' God is using the difficulties to stretch our faith and thereby to strengthen it. Faith must be exercised, and trials provide the opportunity for us to show that we will trust in God even when things are not going well. In this way we learn to persevere, that is, to keep going for a sustained period even when things are difficult. The more we persevere, the more we grow in our faith, and this helps us to mature – to become the kind of people who are steadfast, immovable and always giving themselves to God's work (1 Corinthians 15:58). Those who have been tested and tried are the kind of people whom God can use most effectively.

Perseverance is not a joyless, dull, dutiful characteristic. It is actually joyful, because it can see beyond the present pain and comfort to the bigger picture, appreciating what God is working in us. Bible commentator Derek Tidball notes:

> We respond with joy because we know some of the deeper issues involved which helps us to interpret suffering not as the miserably negative force which others perceive it to be, but as an instrument in the hands of a sovereign, wise and gracious God using it for our good. It is a call to put God into the whole picture of life; the bad times as well as the good.[38]

The apostle Peter adds to our understanding by recognising the purifying effect that trials have on our faith. Trials deliver us from a shallow, self-centred reliance on ourselves, where we are tempted to use God for our own ends, into a faith where we truly depend on him and seek his glory above all. They present us with a kind of test that gives us the opportunity to prove the reality of our faith. He says:

In all this you greatly rejoice, though now for a little while you may have had to suffer grief in all kinds of trials. These have come so that the proven genuineness of your faith – of greater worth than gold, which perishes even though refined by fire – may result in praise, glory and honour when Jesus Christ is revealed.

1 PETER 1:6–7

How, then, does God mediate his help to us?

1   He does so through *the ministry of Jesus as our merciful and faithful high priest*. Jesus himself was tempted by the devil in the wilderness (Matthew 4:1–11). His temptations were real and powerful, yet he resisted the devil and did not sin. But having been tempted as a human being and having overcome, he is now able to communicate to us the grace and strength we need to have victory in the midst of our temptations and trials:

> For we do not have a high priest who is unable to feel sympathy for our weaknesses, but we have one who has been tempted in every way, just as we are – yet he did not sin. Let us then approach God's throne of grace with confidence, so that we may receive mercy and find grace to help us in our time of need.
>
> HEBREWS 4:15–16; see also 2:17–18

Seated now at the right hand of the Father, the risen Jesus is praying for his church, and his intercession is powerful in its effect (Hebrews 7:23–25). Just as he was aware of Peter's forthcoming trial and prayed for him (Luke 22:31–32), so he is aware of our need and prays for us. What is more, as we cry out to him for help, he hears our prayers and pours his grace into our lives, releasing his strength into our weakness (2 Corinthians 12:9).

2   He does so through *the people around us* – those who care for our well-being and who are wise enough to know when we need a little support. The writer of Ecclesiastes puts it so well when he declares that two are better than one: 'If either of them falls down, one can help the other up. But pity anyone who falls and has no one to help them up' (Ecclesiastes 4:10). How valuable it is to have soul friends, people who come alongside us to help and encourage us. Being part of a local church can be a great source of support and practical help. Many people find it helpful also to have the support of a mentor, an individual who knows them well, who walks with them through the challenging periods of life and to whom they

hold themselves accountable. Such a person offers a non-threatening and accepting presence, a prayerful friendship, a listening ear and some wise counsel. They provide a context for honesty and openness, help us to establish good boundaries and ask the kind of questions that keep us on track.

It is not God's will that we fail to complete our discipleship journey or make a shipwreck of our faith. He wants us to succeed and has promised us his help. He is able to keep us from falling and to bring us through whatever trials we face. We can be kept by the power of God (Jude 24–25; 1 Peter 1:5).

## Conversation starters

1 How has your faith been tested? What trials have you faced?
2 Why do you think God allows us to be tested like this? What is his purpose?
3 What do you understand by perseverance? Why is it an important characteristic of a growing disciple?
4 How does Jesus mediate his help to us in our times of trial? What has helped you in your perseverance?
5 Suffering is often compared to being in the refiner's fire (1 Peter 1:7; Malachi 3:2–3). What kind of impurities does God seek to remove from our faith when we go through trials?

## Helpful reading

Jerry Bridges, *Trusting God: Even when life hurts* (NavPress, 2008)
Mags Duggan, *God among the Ruins: Trust and transformation in difficult times* (BRF, 2018)
Tanya Marlow, *Those Who Wait: Finding God in disappointment, doubt and delay* (Malcolm Down Publishing, 2017)
Henri Nouwen, *Can You Drink the Cup?* (Ave Maria Press, 1996)
Patrick Regan with Liza Hoeksma, *When Faith Gets Shaken* (Monarch Books, 2015)

# Staying strong

# 21

# The discipline of stopping

**Be still, and know that I am God; I will be exalted among the nations, I will be exalted in the earth.**
PSALM 46:10

We live in a frantic world, and the pace of life is constantly accelerating. It is easy to get caught up in the mad rush and never have time to stop and think, to take our bearings. Our lives can be so full of endless activity that we forget why we are so busy. We live as if we are on a hamster wheel, moving from one thing to the next without much thought as to the relevance of what we are doing.

Disciples too get caught up in a whirl of worthwhile activity. There seems to be so much to do and so little time to do it. If we are to survive and maintain our joy in God, we need to heed his words in Psalm 46:10, which says, 'Step out of the traffic! Take a long, loving look at me, your High God, above politics, above everything' (MSG). In other words, we must make time to be still and to know that he is God. Our well-being depends on it.

The discipline of stopping is one of those holy habits that we have spoken about already (chapter 16), practices by which we place ourselves in the way of grace. By stepping back from our normal routines we create more space in our lives for God and allow ourselves to connect deeply with him once again, so that we can sustain ourselves over the long haul of life and ministry. I have a definition of stopping that I think is helpful and provides a useful framework for living a God-centred life in a fast-moving world:

> Stopping is pausing for a few minutes, a few hours or a few days to remember who I am and why I am here and to receive strength for the next part of the journey.

If we can learn to live according to this pattern, it will not only save us from burnout and exhaustion but also help us to live from a calm centre.

To practise this discipline we must be willing to press the pause button on our life and give ourselves permission to slow down. Time is a precious commodity, but it is a gift from God, so it is right and proper that we offer it back to him so that he can help us allocate our time accordingly. When we take time to stop, we are not wasting time, since we are stopping for good reason – to better align ourselves with the life of God. The apostle Paul tells us in Ephesians 5:15–17 that we are called to live wisely, using our time well, which means discerning what God wants us to do. To live without such discernment is actually to live foolishly.

We can pause for *a few minutes*, even on the busiest of days. We can begin by committing our way to God, expressing our dependency on him and asking for the Holy Spirit to guide us as we step into a new day. If we have time, we can read the Bible and pray, but as a bare minimum we must connect with God on the basis of our dependency on him in this daily rhythm.

We can pause for *a few hours*, which means planning a short time of study and prayer and quietly seeking God, perhaps once a week. This will also include our Sunday worship as well as the principle of sabbath rest, which we should hold to regularly, yet not in a legalistic way. This becomes our weekly rhythm.

Then we can pause for *a few days*, which means taking time away to consciously seek God for the good of our soul. This might include quarterly quiet days as well as an annual retreat. It will also cover our annual holidays, one of which should be for two weeks, so that we gain the full benefits of stopping. This is our yearly rhythm.

But what are we doing when we stop? What is the purpose? Our definition suggests three important reasons why we stop.

1  We stop in order to *remember who we are* – that is, to remind ourselves yet again of our true identity. In the busyness of life, it is easy to slip back into the old way of thinking that we are what we do. As we have seen already in chapter 6, this leads only to the creation of a false identity. As someone put it shrewdly, 'If I am what I do, when I don't, then I'm not!' We stop to remind ourselves that we are God's deeply loved children, that is who

we are, and our activity should flow out of this secure place. Remember 1 John 3:1? 'See what great love the Father has lavished on us, that we should be called children of God! And that is what we are!' We cannot hear such affirming truth often enough, because we so easily forget it, which is why we discipline ourselves to stop and be reminded of our God-given identity. It is the reason for our confidence, the basis for our security and the inspiration for our service.

2   We stop in order to *remember why we are here*, which is to do God's will. It is vital that we have a clear focus for our activity and that our energies are directed to a strategic goal. So we are always asking God to make clear to us what he would have us do. He has made us for a reason and designed us with his purpose in mind. Paul puts it clearly when he writes, 'For we are God's handiwork, created in Christ Jesus to do good works, which God prepared in advance for us to do' (Ephesians 2:10). Often we have a clear sense of direction, so it is simply a matter of reaffirming that and assessing all that we do in the light of it – which may mean pruning back those activities that do not fit our purpose. At other times we will be less clear and will need to seek fresh guidance for what lies ahead. Always the idea is to come back to what we know to be God's will for us and make sure that we are doing it, no more and no less.

3   We stop in order to *receive strength for the next part of the journey* – that is, to be refreshed and renewed in our calling. Even Jesus discovered that, as he served God and met the demands of people, 'power went out from him' (Luke 6:19; 8:46). We do not have endless resources of energy, compassion or creativity. As we serve others, our inner resources are being depleted, and it is essential that we take time out to rest, be still and be replenished in body, soul and spirit. If not, we shall soon be running on empty and at risk of collapse. That is why Jesus often withdrew to lonely places, both to pray and to rest, and why quiet days and times of retreat should be part of our rhythm of life. Someone put it like this: 'If your output exceeds your input, the shortfall will be your downfall.' Fortunately we need not reach the point of exhaustion. God has promised to give strength to the weary, and that those who wait on the Lord shall renew their strength (Isaiah 40:29–31).

The discipline of stopping is a practical way by which we can structure our life so that we can keep going in ministry and be effective and fruitful over a lifetime of service. Not only that, but it will also ensure that we maintain our joy in God and are prevented from serving simply out of duty and obligation. Stepping aside and taking time out is not a luxury but a necessity. The wise know that if they invest time in taking care of themselves in this way, they will be more effective in the long run and enjoy greater satisfaction in what they do.

## Conversation starters

1   How would you describe your life at the moment? Are you harassed and hurried? Is it time to recalibrate?
2   How do you manage your time? What difference does it make to remember that time is God's gift to you?
3   How can your identity be based more fully on who you are, rather than what you do?
4   Are you clear at the moment about God's will for your life? What is your purpose?
5   How is your energy level right now? What kind of strength do you most need – physical, emotional, mental or moral?

## Helpful reading

Christopher Ash, *Zeal without Burnout: Seven keys to a lifelong ministry of sustainable sacrifice* (The Good Book Company, 2016)
Alicia Britt Chole, *The Sacred Slow: A holy departure from fast faith* (Thomas Nelson, 2017)
John Mark Comer, *The Ruthless Elimination of Hurry: How to stay emotionally healthy and spiritually alive in the chaos of the modern world* (Hodder and Stoughton, 2019)
Tony Horsfall, *Working from a Place of Rest: Jesus and the key to sustaining ministry* (BRF, 2010)
David Kundtz, *Stopping: How to be still when you have to keep going* (Newleaf, 1999)

# 22

# Building resilience

**You need to persevere so that when you have done the will of God, you will receive what he has promised.**
HEBREWS 10:36

Resilience is a relatively modern word, and although it is used a great deal nowadays, you will not find it in the Bible. What you will find is the Greek word *hupomone*, often translated as 'perseverance' or 'endurance'. It is a favourite with the apostle Paul, who regarded it as an essential quality in discipleship, and it is roughly equivalent to our word 'resilience'.

There are many strands of meaning to the idea of resilience, and each gives us an insight into what it means to be resilient. Resilience can be described in the following ways.

- *The ability to bounce back after setbacks, disappointments and seeming defeat.* Joseph is a good example of this form of resilience, as he overcame the difficulties of being sold into slavery in Egypt and then rose to a high position, from which he could later help his own people in a time of famine (Genesis 37—50).

- *The ability to stand firm and even thrive under pressure and opposition.* Nehemiah needed to be resilient as he led the rebuilding of the walls of Jerusalem despite persistent opposition and personal attack from those who didn't want him to succeed (Nehemiah 1—6).

- *The ability to recover from hurt, injury or loss and come back stronger than before.* David saw his home village burnt to the ground by Amalekite raiders, and all the women, children and older people taken hostage. Despite his grief and the blame heaped upon him by his men, he managed to recover his composure and find a way of rescuing his people (1 Samuel 30).

- *The ability to keep going to the end.* The apostle Paul summed up his life in this way: 'I have fought the good fight, I have finished the race, I have kept the faith' (2 Timothy 4:7). Winning a battle, running a race and remaining strong in faith all require great resilience.

- *The ability to adapt to changing circumstances.* The disciples were distraught when Jesus left them, but they found the strength to carry on and adapt to life without him. With the help of the Spirit they took the gospel from Jerusalem to Rome, fulfilling Christ's command to go into all the world.

It seems we are born with a certain amount of resilience. Think of how a premature baby fights for its life and manages to survive, or how despite childhood adversity people manage to overcome against the odds and do well in life. Whole communities show great resilience in the face of natural disasters. Resilience is a wonderful human characteristic that emerges as we face hardship.

At the same time, it is a quality that can be learned and developed. We can increase or build our natural resilience by learning how to manage ourselves through difficulty and cope with our challenges. Added to this, resilience can also be an impartation of divine strength, a gift from God when we most need it. This was Paul's great conviction: 'I can do all this through him who gives me strength' (Philippians 4:13).

Psychologist and Member Care specialist Debbie Hawker has developed a model of resilience that highlights five key factors (or domains) in developing greater resilience. This model, if attended to, will 'provide clarity and help us move around our world without crashing down'.[39] To build maximum resilience, we should establish the building blocks of resilience in all five of the domains. Here is a brief summary of each domain.

## Spiritual

Even secular writers acknowledge that belief in a 'higher power' is a helpful factor in resilience. They also note the importance of prayer and the strength that comes from seeking help from outside of one's own resources. For the believer, our relationship with God is paramount, and the closer we are to him the more resilient we will be. A strong sense of calling helps us to persevere when the going is tough, and a growing trust in the sovereignty of God in all circumstances will enable us to have peace amid turmoil. Psalm 23 is a psalm that breeds such confidence and hope. Karen Carr has paraphrased verse 4 like this:

> Even though I will lose loved ones, have financially lean times, deal with conflicts and misunderstandings, and face health issues, I don't have to be afraid or take control because you've got this [covered]. You'll never leave or abandon me. You are in front of me, beside me, and behind me. No threat or danger is bigger than your protection of me. I can be relaxed… because you are the one at the helm.[40]

## Physical

It is easy in the busyness of life to neglect our body and take it for granted, but if we look after it well, it will mean that we will probably be able to serve longer. The body is the temple of the Holy Spirit (1 Corinthians 6:19–20), and we honour the God who made us by giving attention to our health and well-being. This is not to be selfish but to recognise that 'we have this treasure in jars of clay' (2 Corinthians 4:7), and they are frail and fragile. Therefore, regular exercise is important, as is a good diet and drinking plenty of water. We will want to make sure we get sufficient sleep and establish boundaries in our life so that we can have sufficient time for rest and relaxation. The healthier we are, the more effective we will be, as well as being better able to face the challenges before us.

## Emotional

Some may imagine that to be resilient you must rise above your feelings and not be influenced by them. This is not the case. Resilient people must be aware of and accept their emotions and find healthy ways of expressing them. Getting in touch with our feelings, both positive and negative, is paramount in establishing emotional stability. Disclosing our feelings through talking with a confidant, journaling, creative writing, music or art can be liberating. If we are sad or grieving, it can be helpful to pray and lament, as in many of the psalms, so that our grief, loss and anger can find expression. We should not be afraid to cry. Weeping is healthy and healing and not a sign of weakness or lack of backbone. Men especially may need to overcome their fear of crying. Likewise we should not hesitate to share our joys and celebrate when good things happen.

## Cognitive

How we think is crucial in interpreting what happens to us. We must adopt a mindset in which God is in control and working out his perfect will in our lives. Our concept of God is vital – we should see him as a merciful and compassionate God who loves us passionately and wants what is best for us. When bad things happen, it is not that he is angry with us or punishing us in some way. He will never leave us or abandon us, but he is right there with us in the hard times. This is where a theology of suffering can hold us firm when questions and doubts arise and we are asking 'Why, Lord?' (see chapter 29).

The mind is a battlefield, and Satan seeks to sow negative and destructive ideas into our thinking so that we go astray. This is why we must 'take captive every thought' and bring it under submission to the truth of scripture (2 Corinthians 10:4–5). It is also why scripture gives such a high priority to the renewing of our minds (Romans 12:2), which means replacing our old, negative thought patterns with the truth of who we are in Christ and all that he has promised to do for us. Memorising and meditating on scripture will help with this, but it takes time and is an ongoing work of grace.

## Social

Resilient people do not try to go it alone; they know the wisdom of surrounding themselves with good friends, mentors and specialist helpers. Such social support prevents us from being lonely and therefore more vulnerable to temptation; it also adds to our wisdom when it comes to decision-making. Having a church family can be really helpful, for it gives to everyone (young or old, married or single) a place where we belong and can safely ask for help. Meaningful fellowship, where we are open and honest about our struggles and can receive prayer and ministry, is a major asset in building resilience. Friendships are vitally important, but it requires time to build and nurture such relationships. Such time is always well spent. Scripture wisely says, 'Two are better than one, because they have a good return for their labour: if either of them falls down, one can help the other up. But pity anyone who falls and has no one to help them up' (Ecclesiastes 4:9–10).

As we pay attention to how we are doing in each of these five domains, we can significantly increase our ability to weather the storms of life. To be resilient is not to be untroubled by the challenge of life or to somehow rise above the difficulties that trouble others; it is to face exactly the same adversities that are common to humanity and yet, by the grace of God, to come through them victoriously.

## Conversation starters

1  Who do you know who has shown resilience in their life? What were their main characteristics?
2  Where have you needed to show resilience in your own life? What have you learned from your experience?
3  Which Bible characters speak about resilience for you? What scriptures come to mind that encourage resilience?
4  How might having a living faith increase our resilience?
5  Of the five domains of resilience identified by Debbie Hawker, which do you most need to work on?

## Helpful reading

Justine Allain-Chapman, *Resilient Pastors: The role of adversity in healing and growth* (SPCK, 2012)
Kirsten Birkett, *Resilience: A spiritual project* (Latimer Trust, 2016)
Jane Clarke and John Nicholson, *Resilience: Bounce back from whatever life throws at you* (Crimson, 2012)
Debbie Duncan, *The Art of Daily Resilience: How to develop a durable spirit* (Monarch, 2017)
Tony Horsfall and Debbie Hawker, *Resilience in Life and Faith: Finding your strength in God* (BRF, 2019)

# 23

# The importance of self-care

**Then, because so many people were coming and going that they did not even have a chance to eat, he said to them, 'Come with me by yourselves to a quiet place and get some rest.'**
MARK 6:31

To some who are busily serving God, speaking about self-care may seem like a contradiction, a negation of the basic call of the gospel to deny ourselves and seek instead the good of others. The very idea of caring for oneself may be considered selfish, a concession to our self-centred, pampered society. Shouldn't Christians be made of sterner stuff? Isn't there a world to be won, and not much time in which to do it?

There is no doubt that discipleship sometimes requires us to place the needs of others before our own, but to do this continually and without thought for our own legitimate needs is actually a dangerous approach. Over time it can lead to weariness, exhaustion and eventual burnout. To sustain ourselves over a lifetime of service, we must learn to care for ourselves so that we can continue to care for others.

Jesus himself was often hard-pressed by the relentless demands upon him, but a close inspection of the gospel accounts shows that he was careful to manage his own needs as well. We see him sitting by Sychar's well and taking a breather, enjoying a well-earned rest (John 4:6). He often chose to be alone, seeking the restorative balance of solitude and prayer and refusing to be at everyone's beck and call (Mark 1:35–37). He found personal space in being in the countryside, walking by the lake and withdrawing to the mountains. He kept the regular discipline of sabbath and worship (Luke 4:16) and re-energised himself by being with friends whose company he enjoyed and whose home was a safe place, such as the family at Bethany (Mark 7:24; Luke 10:38).

More than that, we see that Jesus taught his disciples to follow a similar pattern, urging them to step aside from the demands of ministry to be alone with him (Mark 6:31). His invitation to them – and to all of us – was to find a place of rest out of which their activity could flow. Eugene Peterson has captured the heart of the Master in his paraphrase of Matthew 11:28–30:

> Are you tired? Worn out? Burned out on religion? Come to me. Get away with me and you'll recover your life. I'll show you how to take a real rest. Walk with me and work with me – watch how I do it. Learn the unforced rhythms of grace. I won't lay anything heavy or ill-fitting on you. Keep company with me and you'll learn to live freely and lightly.
> MATTHEW 11:28–30 (MSG)

This invitation resonates deeply with many modern-day disciples who find themselves overcommitted and under-resourced. It reminds us that it is not God's will that we should drive ourselves into the ground until we break down and can no longer serve. His call is to a life of partnership with him and to a way of working that is both enjoyable and effective.

How, then, can we care for ourselves in ways that are consistent with our calling to serve God and to be true disciples?

1  We can *review our energy level* and notice when we are becoming depleted emotionally, physically or mentally. Human beings have finite resources, and we cannot keep giving out without taking in. We need rest and refreshment so that we can be renewed, and if we deny ourselves the necessary time and space to refuel, we place ourselves at risk. As someone wisely said, 'If your output exceeds your input, the shortfall will be your downfall.' Taking a regular day off, having planned breaks and annual holidays and not burning the candle at both ends will help to keep us motivated and enjoying what we do.

2  We can be more *aware of our load and our limits*. None of us has an infinite capacity. Just as an electric socket will burn a fuse if it is overloaded, so human beings who continually push themselves beyond their God-given limits are prone to burn out. Recognise the signs when you are overloaded – headaches, minor illness, irritability, sleep problems and so on. Your body will tell you when it is overloaded, and a wise person will make adjustments accordingly by cutting back until equilibrium is restored. As Richard Swenson has written, 'It is God the Creator who has made limits,

and it is the same God who placed them within us for our protection. We exceed them at our peril.'[41]

3   We can learn to *establish margins and boundaries*. We establish boundaries by learning to say 'No' to those invitations, opportunities or demands that might tip us over the edge of our capacity and capability. We do not have to say 'Yes' to everything, only to those things that God is calling us to. We need to develop a prayerful discernment so that we are not pushed beyond the call of God. People-pleasers may find this hard, but it is essential we learn this discipline, otherwise our lives will be overrun with tasks that are not God-given. For instance, if we closely guard our day of rest, it will ensure that we have the margin we need to keep our relationship with God fresh and alive, and also have time for ourselves.

4   We can choose to be *kind to ourselves*. Many of us show far more grace to others than we do to ourselves. Being kind to ourselves is to give ourselves permission to slow down, take a break and consider our own well-being. As a priority we need to rest and to make sure we get sufficient sleep, as this is the main way we are restored. If we are sleep-deprived, we will not function well. Then we need time to relax, to unwind and chill out, and let the cares of life drift away for a while. The human body was not meant to live continually under strain, and we must build into our lives ways by which we can relax physically, emotionally and mentally. As we find our energy returning, we can then enjoy some recreation. Times of fun and play help us to let off steam and are key to preserving our health and well-being amid heavy demands and responsibilities.

It should be clear that in encouraging self-care we are not encouraging people to be lazy or irresponsible, to neglect their duty or to be half-hearted in their discipleship. We want people to give their all for the cause of Christ, but to do so in a way that does not place them at risk of burnout or damaging to their health.

Our call is to steward our souls wisely, because we cannot give what we do not have, and if we continually transgress our limits we do violence to ourselves. Spiritual director Stephen W. Smith has said:

> We forfeit our souls every single time we choose to drain ourselves and not replenish ourselves; run on empty rather than stopping and intentionally doing the things that will bring us life; burnout rather than

live meaningful, significant, and impactful lives that are enjoyable and life-giving to others.'[42]

What we are seeking is to establish a rhythm of life where we are both taking in and giving out, breathing in (receiving from God) and then breathing out (serving others). To achieve such a rhythm is a continual challenge in a world that incessantly demands more of us, and where the needs are constantly increasing and ever before us. Yet with care and prayerful dependency on God, such a rhythm is not only desirable but also achievable.

## Conversation starters

1   How do you react to the idea of self-care? What shapes your thinking about the importance of looking after yourself?
2   How do you respond to the words of Jesus in Matthew 11:28–30 as given in *The Message*? What words or phrases strike you most, and why?
3   Of the four ways by which we may care for ourselves, which seems the most important to you at the present time?
4   What does your rhythm of life look like? Is it time to make some changes? If so, how would you like to make these adjustments?
5   What might prevent you from taking better care of yourself in the future? What will help you to live a more balanced life?

## Helpful reading

Fil Anderson, *Running on Empty: Contemplative spirituality for overachievers* (Waterbrook Press, 2004)
Peter Scazzero, *Emotionally Healthy Spirituality: Unleash a revolution in your life in Christ* (Thomas Nelson, 2006)
Stephen W. Smith, *Embracing Soul Care: Making space for what matters most* (Kregel, 2006)
Paul Swann, *Sustaining Leadership: You are more important than your ministry* (BRF, 2018)
Richard Swenson, *Margin: Restoring emotional, physical, financial, and time reserves to overloaded lives* (NavPress, 2004)

# 24

# Practising sabbath

**Then [Jesus] said to them, 'The Sabbath was made for man, not man for the Sabbath. So the Son of Man is Lord even of the Sabbath.'**
MARK 2:27–28

If we are to stay strong over the years of following Jesus, so that we finish as enthusiastically as we began, it will be because we have learned the importance of self-care. A significant part of that is to incorporate the practice of sabbath rest into our rhythm of life. God has given us permission to rest so that we have time for our relationship with him (and others) and to nourish our souls.

To understand why sabbath is important to us today, we need to go back to the Old Testament origins of this special day. In the Genesis account of creation we read:

> By the seventh day God had finished the work he had been doing; so on the seventh day he rested from all his work. Then God blessed the seventh day and made it holy, because on it he rested from all the work of creating that he had done.
> GENESIS 2:2–3

Here we see that rest is good. It is woven into the fabric of creation, into the rhythm of life itself. One of God's blessings to us is this gift of rest. We are not machines that can operate non-stop, but human beings who need to pause and rest for the sake of our health and well-being.

Why did God rest? Not because he was tired, for the everlasting God does not grow tired or weary (Isaiah 40:28). He rested because he wanted to give us an example of how we too can rest from our work. Work is important, but it should not define our existence. If we are to work well, it will be because we are rested. By pausing in this way, God showed us that to rest is holy. We stop our work because we are created beings who need to be refreshed and renewed, and this pleases him.

What is worth pointing out here is that Adam, who was created on day six, began his life with sabbath, the seventh day and a day of rest. He started with a holiday! This is instructive for us, because he did not have to earn his rest. It was given not as a reward for his hard work but as a preparation for the work which was to come. This is an important spiritual principle which runs throughout all the Christian life and undergirds all God's dealings with us. This is the way of grace, where God always acts first and we respond to what he has already done. He provides, then we receive; he initiates, and we respond. Thus the Chinese leader Watchman Nee (1903–72) said insightfully, 'Whereas God worked six days and then enjoyed his Sabbath rest, Adam began his life with the Sabbath; for God works before he rests, while man must first enter into God's rest, and then alone can he work.'[43]

When, in the busyness of our lives, we cease from our activity and choose to rest, we are following the principle of sabbath and establishing again in our hearts our understanding of the way of grace. We can rest because the work is God's, and he has assured us that if we take time out in this way and honour him, he will make sure our work does not suffer.

The importance of sabbath is further underlined by the way in which it became enshrined in the ten commandments, the basis for covenantal living in the Old Testament. The first account of the giving of the commandments takes us back to the creation event and the fact that God rested, enjoining us to do likewise by limiting our work to six days and keeping the seventh for rest and worship (Exodus 20:8–11). The second account reminds the people that although they were once slaves in Egypt, they are slaves no more. As God's people they have been redeemed and are free to rest on the sabbath, a celebration of their salvation and a privilege they could never enjoy as slaves (Deuteronomy 5:12–15). The practice of sabbath, therefore, first brings us into line with the rhythm of creation as the best way to live, then reminds us that we are not to be enslaved to our work or personal ambitions, but to be centred upon God and his grace towards us.

At the time of Jesus, sabbath observance had degenerated into legalism and the keeping of many rules and regulations. This was why he deliberately contravened many of the Pharisaic traditions associated with the sabbath. But he was not against the sabbath itself. His own custom was to worship on the sabbath, and he explicitly declared it to have been given for the benefit of all (Luke 4:16; Mark 2:27). The apostle Paul also warned of the dangers of legalism surrounding the sabbath (Colossians 2:16–17; Romans 14:4–6), while the book of Hebrews shows us that sabbath rest is ultimately found only in Christ (Hebrews 4:9–11). The early church seems to have seen its natural fulfilment in the first day of the week (the Lord's Day), when they met for worship and remembered the resurrection (Revelation 1:10; 1 Corinthians 16:2).

So how are we to keep sabbath?

It is important to remember that it is not so much about a particular day as a spiritual principle – that of stopping our work and setting aside one day each week for the purpose of resting and worshipping God. Then it is also important to recognise that it is not about a legalistic observance but a spiritual practice – something we choose to do because we want to, not something we are forced to do and will be punished for if we don't. It is a gift given to us for our well-being, and it is not intended to be a joyless burden or unwanted inconvenience.

Having said that, how then might we incorporate the practice of sabbath into our lives today? Theologian Marva J. Dawn, in her book *Keeping the Sabbath Wholly*, suggests four aspects to sabbath-keeping that can provide a helpful framework for us as we seek to incorporate this discipline into our rhythm of life.

1  *Ceasing*: we are invited to stop our work and are freed from the need to produce or achieve. We are called to rest in the sovereignty of God.

2  *Resting*: we are invited to rest physically, emotionally and spiritually as we trust in God and worship him.

3  *Embracing*: we are invited to take our place among God's people through corporate worship and to renew ourselves in the purpose that God has for our lives.

4  *Feasting*: we are invited to celebrate all that is ours in Christ Jesus and to enjoy ourselves in fun and festivity so that we can be refreshed in body, soul and spirit.

Dawn notes that to 'keep the sabbath holy' means to recognise that the rhythm of six days of work and one day of ceasing work is written into the very core of our beings. The great benefit of this practice is that 'we learn to let God take care of us – not by becoming passive and lazy, but in the freedom of giving up our feeble attempts to be God in our own lives'.[44] To practise sabbath requires a degree of faith, since we have to trust that if we are not working, God will take care of us.

The actual practice of sabbath will vary from person to person as we seek to incorporate the principle into our unique set of circumstances and individual lifestyles. There is no set day and no set pattern. We are free to develop the practice as we feel best for us at this point in our lives. It may look different when we have a young family to when we are retired, for instance, but the key thing is this: keeping sabbath is part of God's wisdom for our health, well-being and spiritual formation. It is his good gift to us, and we neglect it to our detriment.

## Conversation starters

1  What has been your experience of sabbath so far in your Christian life?
2  How does the recognition that sabbath is a creation ordinance help your understanding of its importance?
3  Why do you think sabbath is so neglected today, even among believers?
4  How does seeing sabbath as both a principle and a practice help us in our application of it today?
5  How might the insights of Marva J. Dawn inform the way you practise sabbath in the future?

## Helpful reading

Dan B. Allender, *Sabbath* (Thomas Nelson, 2009)
Lynne M. Baab, *Sabbath Keeping: Finding freedom in the rhythms of rest* (IVP, 2005)
Marva J. Dawn, *Keeping the Sabbath Wholly: Ceasing, resting, embracing, feasting* (Eerdmans, 1989)
Keri Wyatt Kent, *Rest: Living in sabbath simplicity* (Zondervan, 2009)
Wayne Muller, *Sabbath Rest: Restoring the sacred rhythm of rest* (Lion, 1999)

# 25

# A spiritual health check

**But the Lord God called to the man, 'Where are you?'**
GENESIS 3:9

Often in an unfamiliar city I will look for an information point and a map of the general layout of the place. Usually the map will have a red arrow pointing to a specific location, with the words 'You are here'. Once you have found that, you can find your bearings and work out how to get to where you want to be.

In the spiritual life it is important to be able to locate ourselves. It is always worth taking time out occasionally to check on our progress and reflect on what is happening in our life, otherwise we can drift without our realising it. I find it helpful to ask myself five simple questions.

## Who am I?

This is the question of identity, which is important because identity determines behaviour. How we see ourselves will influence how we behave. Part of our spiritual journey is to come to an understanding that our identity is based upon what God says of us, not on anything else – for example, what we do, what we have, what we achieve or what others think of us. The declaration of the Bible is clear: we are God's deeply loved children.

The apostle John was secure in his identity as 'the disciple whom Jesus loved' (John 13:23; 19:26; 20:2; 21:7, 20). He did not, however, regard this as something unique to himself, but as a reality for us all. He writes, 'See what great love the Father has lavished on us, that we should be called children of God! And that is what we are!' (1 John 3:1). This is not a status we have achieved, but a standing bestowed upon us. We are objects of the divine love, and nothing can change that. It is who we really are. Once this truth dawns upon us, it becomes the foundation for how we live and grow. Knowing ourselves to be loved, we are free to admit our shortcomings and to change. Knowing ourselves to be loved, we are liberated to love others even as we have been loved. Knowing ourselves to be loved, we are increasingly released from fear and worry because we know that God is watching over us.

Brennan Manning, one of the great exponents of this truth, quotes his friend John Egan as saying, 'Define yourself radically as one beloved by God. This is your true self. Every other identity is an illusion.'[45]

## Where am I?

The spiritual life is often compared to a journey, indeed a sacred journey or pilgrimage. The psalmist said, 'Blessed are those whose strength is in you, whose hearts are set on pilgrimage' (Psalm 84:5). To journey well, we must be aware of where we are and where we want to be.

Life itself is like a journey, and it is important to know where we are on that journey. There are different stages to our lives, and each stage has its own needs, opportunities and challenges. Such a stage comes in our 20s as we enter adulthood and face many big choices – what career to follow, what relationships to invest in, where to live and so on. Midlife (see chapter 27) is another major transition requiring great wisdom. Retirement and beyond confronts us with the need to adapt to the ageing process and to consider how we can use our remaining time well. Each new stage requires us to adjust accordingly to the new situation.

Then there is the journey of discipleship, described by Eugene Peterson as 'a long obedience in the same direction'.[46] Having chosen to follow Jesus, we are often faced with 'crossroad moments' when we have to choose again to follow God's will for our life. The path of obedience is never straightforward. There are twists and turns, ups and downs, detours and roadblocks, hold-ups and delays. We are continually being asked if we will be faithful to our calling.

Intertwined with these two journeys is a third – the journey of transformation, which refers to the way God is forming us into the likeness of his Son (Romans 8:29; Galatians 4:19). We are called to change, to grow and to mature, a process of becoming that is intrinsically tied to both our life stage and the circumstances of our lives as we seek to follow Jesus.

# How am I?

We need not become overly introspective as we answer this question, but it is wise to consider how we are doing in each of these domains – physically, mentally, emotionally and spiritually. In the busyness of life, it is easy to neglect ourselves. Indeed, for some, the notion of self-care may seem selfish and unspiritual. However, rightly looking after ourselves enables us to sustain ourselves in service of others over the long haul.

- *Physically* – the body is the temple of the Holy Spirit (1 Corinthians 6:19). How am I looking after it, especially when it comes to diet, exercise, sleep and general lifestyle?

- *Mentally* – the mind is often a battlefield. How do I manage my thoughts? How can I detect, and respond to, signs of depression and anxiety?

- *Emotionally* – we should neither suppress our emotions nor be a prisoner to them. Am I able to cry? Do I laugh and have fun? Emotional balance leads to stability of life.

- *Spiritually* – our relationship with God is never static, and the spiritual life ebbs and flows. How do I nourish my soul? Am I aware of my inner life and the state of my relationship with God?

# Why am I?

This question brings us back to our purpose in life. Without a sense of purpose life becomes meaningless, and without a sense of direction we lack fulfilment. God has plans for our lives. Jeremiah is often quoted in this regard, when God says, 'I know the plans I have for you… plans to prosper you and not to harm you, plans to give you hope and a future' (Jeremiah 29:11).

Every now and then we need to pause to see if we are still living according to that purpose, or to consider if God may have a change of direction for us. This assumes, of course, that we are willing to do God's will and to place that before our own desires and ambitions. Throughout a life of discipleship there will be moments when we surrender ourselves afresh to God, yielding our right to self-determination and offering ourselves again so that his purposes for us can come to pass.

# Whose am I?

The final question is, in fact, the most important one. It reminds us that we are not our own, that we belong to God. The apostle Paul says, 'You are not your own; you were bought at a price. Therefore honour God with your bodies' (1 Corinthians 6:19–20). Each of us has a debt of gratitude to God and to Christ, who willingly gave his life that we might be set free. We have been redeemed at great cost (1 Peter 1:18–19), and this knowledge motivates us to offer ourselves willingly back to God, not out of duty but out of love.

Often we will experience a struggle within us when it comes to this surrender. At such moments we remember that surrender to God is always surrender to love, the giving of ourselves to the one who loves us with a boundless, unchanging love. He only wants what is best for us, and we should not fear to yield ourselves to him. The words of the great hymn by Isaac Watts (1674–1748), a meditation on the cross, have fired the passion in the hearts of many:

*Were the whole realm of nature mine,*
*that were a present far too small.*
*Love so amazing, so divine,*
*demands my soul, my life, my all.*

## Conversation starters

1  How well is your identity grounded in what God says about you? Where else are you tempted to look for your worth and value?
2  How do you answer the question, 'Where am I?'
3  How are you doing in each of the four domains of well-being – physical, mental, emotional and spiritual?
4  What do you understand to be God's purpose for your life? Are you keeping to it?
5  How does the knowledge that you were bought at a price affect how you live?

# Helpful reading

Brennan Manning, *Abba's Child: The cry of the heart for intimate belonging* (NavPress, 1994)

John Ortberg, *Soul Keeping: Caring for the most important part of you* (Zondervan, 2014)

Eugene Peterson, *A Long Obedience in the Same Direction: Discipleship in an instant society* (IVP, 1980)

Stephen W. Smith, *Soul Custody: Choosing to care for the one and only you* (David C. Cook, 2010)

# Living with mystery

# 26

# Stages of faith

**Blessed are those whose strength is in you, whose hearts are set on pilgrimage. As they pass through the Valley of Baka, they make it a place of springs; the autumn rains also cover it with pools. They go from strength to strength, till each appears before God in Zion.**
PSALM 84:5–7

I love the idea of the Christian life as a journey. It suggests to me steady progress made over a lifetime, with a sense of adventure and discovery. It also brings to mind the idea that there are stages along the way and that knowing where we are at any given moment can help us enjoy the journey more.

Many years ago, I was introduced to a book called *The Critical Journey* by Janet Hagberg and Robert Guelich.[47] Based on their own experience and their research with other believers, they attempt to identify some of the milestones on the journey of faith. The model they propose is the one I have found most helpful, since it describes my own experience and fits comfortably with the scriptural picture of the Christian life. They suggest six key stages, which I summarise here.

1   *Recognition of God*: this is the stage when we first become aware of God. This may happen through a natural awareness of his existence that has always been with us, through a sense of awe as we encounter him in the world he made or through a sense of need for forgiveness or help with the problems of life. In fact, all three of these factors may be involved in our journey to faith. At this early stage, faith is childlike and enthusiastic.

2   *The life of discipleship*: once we come to faith, we get involved with a group of other believers, and we begin to learn more about God from what we are taught. We learn what we have to do to become part of the group and happily follow a leader we respect. We begin to identify our gifts and special contribution and may seek responsibility. Faith is secure

and we carry a sense of rightness about what we believe. We are happy to be a good follower.

3   *The productive life*: faith is now expressed by working for God, and, having found our unique place in the faith community, we take on more responsibility, perhaps even coming into a leadership position. The emphasis is on productivity and success; roles, titles and recognition may be important. This may be the time when we take on further training and, for some, make decisions about full-time ministry.

4   *The journey inward*: here faith is rediscovering God. The move inward may be brought about by a feeling of exhaustion or burnout, since the productive life stage is very demanding physically. Instinctively we sense there must be a better way to live, and we begin to look for something deeper and based more on being and less on doing. It may also come about through a crisis of faith and be accompanied by a loss of certainty. There may well be a search for a new direction, not necessarily answers. Having lived so much in the outer world, we now give our attention to the inner world. God is released from the box of our own understanding and tradition.

4a   *The wall*: although strictly part of stage 4, this experience is deemed so critical that it is treated separately. 'The wall' represents the place of challenge, where our will meets God's will face to face. We decide anew whether we are willing to surrender and let God direct our lives. It is a pivotal moment in the journey, but often a place of mystery and is different for everyone. All our defences and false identities are exposed, and the barriers we have made between ourselves and God begin to crumble. We may well resist the pain involved, but if we are willing to pass through the wall it will become a time of healing, forgiveness, acceptance by God and awareness of his unconditional love. Stillness and silence may become part of our journey. Interestingly, this stage often seems to coincide with the choppy waters of midlife, when we transition from the first half of life to the second.

5   *The journey outward*: faith is now surrendering to God more fully, and, drawn closer to him through his unconditional love, we have a renewed sense of calling and ministry. Working from a place of rest within ourselves, we are energised to focus now on the needs of others, but from a place of selfless love, not desire for success. We are learning to abide

in Christ, as described by Jesus in John 15 with the allegory of the vine and the branches. I like to call this stage 'the fruitful life', since it is characterised by dependency on God and working *with* God, in contrast to 'the productive life' (stage 3), which is characterised by working *for* God and the tendency to operate through self-effort.

6 *The life of love*: faith is now reflecting God as we begin to see Christ formed within us and live in total obedience to his will. Wisdom we have gained on the journey is used to help others, we have a greater detachment from material things and we are freed from the stressful striving for position and power of earlier stages. There is a greater contentment about us, and we are genuinely compassionate towards others.

Hagberg and Guelich are quick to point out that these stages are very fluid and that there is a lot of movement between them. Sometimes we move forward; at other times we may regress. They also describe how we can get stuck at any particular stage, and point out the need for spiritual mentoring, particularly if we are to move from stage 3 onwards, and most crucially when we are facing the wall.

This concept of the Christian life as a journey, with various developmental stages, is important for church leaders to grasp, for both their own spiritual growth and that of those in their care. How do we help people to keep moving forward, and what kind of pastoral support do they need along the way? How might church programmes be shaped by this? The danger is that we assume that everyone is at the same stage and that a one-size-fits-all approach will work. Clearly those going through the turmoil of hitting the wall will need a more person-centred approach.

Churches that are heavily goal-oriented, with a large programme to service and maintain, may well have a vested interest in keeping people at the productive life stage. They need people to be busy and active to keep the show on the road, and therefore may not welcome an emphasis on the inner life or recognise the need to let people step back a little in order to find a deeper place in God. The danger of this is that many of the most committed disciples will either burn out or drop out. If, however, we can guide people through the transition from the productive life to the fruitful life, we will find that we have a group of experienced people who are more effective in what they do and who are enjoying their life in God more than ever. That can only be a blessing to a congregation.

# Conversation starters

1   How does this model of spiritual development work for you?
    When you look back over your life can you see yourself in any of these
    stages?
2   Where do you think you are at present?
3   At this stage in your discipleship, what kind of support do you need?
    What challenges are you facing and what opportunities do you see
    ahead of you?
4   Why does the experience of the wall seem to be so pivotal?
5   How do you think churches can help people through some of the
    transitions that are part of normal spiritual growth, in particular when
    facing the wall?

# Helpful reading

Peter Feldmeier, *The Developing Christian: Spiritual growth through the life
    cycle* (Paulist Press, 2007)
Janet O. Hagberg and Robert A. Guelich, *The Critical Journey: Stages in the
    life of faith* (Sheffield Publishing Company, 2005)
Alan Jamieson, *A Churchless Faith: Faith journeys beyond the churches*
    (SPCK, 2002)
Peter Scazzero, *Emotionally Healthy Spirituality: Unleash a revolution in
    your life in Christ* (Thomas Nelson, 2006)

# 27

# Discipleship through midlife

**I was young and now I am old.**
PSALM 37:25

Midlife is the period of transition between the first half of life ('I was young') and the second half ('and now I am old'), a time of deep personal evaluation as we reflect on the past and prepare for the future. It may or may not involve a crisis, but it will almost certainly involve experiencing some inner turmoil and navigating some choppy waters. There is both danger and opportunity during this transition – the danger of making bad choices but also the opportunity to discover new and exciting possibilities for our life.

Discipleship is a call to follow Jesus through the changing scenes of our lives and to work out what discipleship means at any given stage in our life. Spiritually, midlife is a crucial passage involving a fundamental reassessment of what we believe and how we live. It is a critical time for spiritual formation and soul-making when it is good to have the help of a trusted mentor or soul friend.

Midlife normally occurs anywhere between the ages of 40–60 and can last for a few years or as long as a decade. It is often triggered by a precipitating event, such as a significant birthday, children leaving home, a redundancy, a divorce or the experience of burnout. Sometimes the sudden realisation that life is passing us by and that there is now more behind us than ahead of us starts us thinking more deeply. It is always worth investing time to stop and think about our life and its future direction. Psalm 90:12 says, 'Teach us to number our days, that we may gain a heart of wisdom.' It is helpful to look at our midlife journey from three perspectives.

## Looking backward: reviewing the past

Nostalgia is a natural part of growing older. It feels as if we need to find our roots and that we can only move forward if we have pieced together the past. For some this means finding out more about their childhood and early years. This may involve visiting places we once knew and reconnecting with friends we left behind. For a few it may mean a search for birth parents or unravelling family history. All of this helps us to answer the questions 'How did I get here?' and 'What events have shaped me?'

At the same time we need to make peace with our past, coming to terms with how life has worked out for us. Some may have seen their dreams fulfilled; others may have experienced only disappointment – the breakdown of a marriage, childlessness, a career that didn't work out, the onset of poor health, the realisation that we may be single all our life, and so on. Acceptance of the reality is crucial to moving forward. Seeing God's hand in all the events of life can help with this process, as can being willing to forgive and let go of any sadness or regret (Romans 8:28; Genesis 45:5–8; 50:20).

Midlife is naturally a time for evaluating what we have achieved so far and what we hope to achieve in the future. By this time we will have a more realistic assessment of our gifts and capabilities, and we have the opportunity to change direction if we wish.

## Looking inward: adapting to the present

Midlife is a time of change internally. We are growing as people, and growth necessitates change. The first half of life is about achievement, building a life and getting ahead. This means we live in the external world, at pace and with little time for reflection. Exhaustion and the threat of burnout call us to a better way of living and the nurturing of our inner life. This movement towards interiority helps to bring balance to our lives and to find our identity not in what we do but in who we are and who we are becoming.

There may also be a growing desire to be true to ourselves and not simply to live up to the expectations of others, or even be chained to the image we have created for ourselves. We may become more aware of our 'false self' (the persona we have created to get by in life, which is not totally who we really are) and long to be more fully our 'true self in God' (the person God made us to be, and who we know we really are). This movement towards greater authenticity and integrity is characteristic of midlife and an integral part of our spiritual growth.

Midlife is a period of great soul-searching, as we question previously held beliefs, especially about God, the Bible, suffering and the church. For some, this is deeply disorientating, but again it is part of coming to a mature faith. Often this will mean an acceptance of the mystery of God (that we can never fathom all he does) and a growing sense of the need for trust in his goodness and grace, even when we don't understand. This is the movement from knowing to not-knowing, and, although disturbing, it is a well-worn path and not to be feared.

## Looking forward: anticipating the future

It is helpful in midlife to pause and ask God to show us his direction for the future. It may be that we build on what has gone before, or it could be that we sense a new direction altogether. It always requires faith to step into something new, and midlife for many is a time to take bold steps.

What we are looking for as we approach the second half of life is the coming together of who we are (our personality and gifting) with what we do (our work, ministry or calling). When these two fit well together, we will be at our most efficient and effective, we will be operating out of who we are and our work will be more enjoyable and fulfilling. Discovering the passion within us, and the deep desire of our heart, can help us in discerning God's will for the next phase. Our most significant contribution is likely to be in the second half of life, so it is worth taking time to think carefully and prayerfully about God's will for us. Ideally we are looking for our vocation – the particular work that God has for us to do in the next phase of our life. Frederick Buechner beautifully sums this up for us when he says, 'The place God calls you to is the place where your deep gladness and the world's deep hunger meet.'[48]

We may also find ourselves drawn at this stage to mentoring and developing others. This may be informally or in a more structured way, but such an investment in the next generation will be part of our legacy, the fruit of our life and experience. It is worthwhile receiving training in this area if this is to be part of your calling.

We will all know people for whom midlife involved making wrong choices and losing their way. It need not be so, but most of us will need some help as we navigate the choppy waters of our midlife passage. Seeking help is not a sign of weakness but of wisdom. Don't be afraid to look for guidance when the time comes; it may well be the making of you.

## Conversation starters

1   Do you recognise any of the signs of midlife in yourself at present? What are they?
2   How well are you connected to your past? How has it shaped you? What questions do you have?
3   What internal changes do you see taking place within you? How do you relate to the three perspectives described here?
4   What feelings do you have as you look towards the future? Do you have any sense of how God may be leading you?
5   What kind of legacy do you wish to leave? How might you help the next generation?

## Helpful reading

Frederick Buechner, *Listening to Your Life* (HarperSanFrancisco, 1992)
Tony Horsfall, *Spiritual Growth in a Time of Change: Following God in midlife* (BRF, 2016)
Sue Monk Kidd, *When the Heart Waits: Spiritual direction for life's sacred questions* (HarperCollins, 1992)
Richard Rohr, *Falling Upward: A spirituality for the two halves of life* (Jossey-Bass, 2011)
Sheridan Voysey, *The Making of Us: Who we can become when life doesn't go as planned* (Thomas Nelson, 2019)

# 28

# Mystery

**Can you fathom the mysteries of God? Can you probe the limits of the Almighty? They are higher than the heavens above – what can you do? They are deeper than the depths below – what can you know?**
JOB 11:7–8

Having spent four years at Bible College and graduated with an honours degree in theology, I entered Christian ministry with a fair degree of confidence that I was intellectually prepared for the challenge. After all, I had studied Christian doctrine and completed modules on systematic theology. I felt I was ready to answer any question that came my way.

Ministry took us overseas to Malaysia and eight exciting years establishing churches in the coastal towns of the island of Borneo. Our two children were born there, and it was a good time for us as a family. We returned to England in 1983, and I began pastoral ministry in a local church, which had its ups and downs, but on the whole was good. All the way through I faithfully taught that which I had been taught, and it seemed to work. Then a personal crisis came along that rocked – and nearly sank – my theological boat.

The crisis was this: as they came to the end of their teenage years, both my children decided to stop attending church. It was a deep blow to my faith, because I couldn't understand why God had allowed it to happen. I had lived my life according to the biblical maxim that 'those who honour me I will honour' (1 Samuel 2:30). I did not ask much from God, but I did expect that since we had honoured him with our whole lives, our children would follow in the faith. When they didn't, I felt that God had let me down, and badly. It seemed unfair that those who had not sacrificed as we had should see their children on fire for God, whereas we who had given our all had the pain of seeing them turn away. I was angry with God and wanted to quit.

Through the counsel of a wise spiritual director I began to examine my basic assumption, and I realised that I was reading into the promise what I wanted to get out of it. In many ways God has honoured me, and the story with my children is not yet over. However, it made me question many things I had previously taken for granted, and my understanding of God began to change. Whereas before I felt I knew exactly what God was like and could predict how he would act, now I realise it is not possible to do that. God is far too great to fit into anyone's theological box, no matter how refined their theology or how powerful their intellect. I was introduced to the idea of mystery, that God is beyond our understanding or logic and that we may not always be able to fathom what he does. I still don't understand why my hopes for my children have so far not been realised, but I have become content to not understand and choose rather to trust that God knows what he is doing.

In the scientific and rational age in which we live it is easy to think we can analyse God and systematise his ways, but that is a big mistake. If we could understand God, we would be greater than him. Our tiny, finite minds cannot possibly compute all there is to know about an infinite God or his ways. This means that sometimes we have to be content with mystery and comfortable with not knowing. The apostle Paul, basing his prayer on Isaiah 40:13 and Job 41:11, makes this exclamation in the book of Romans:

> Oh, the depth of the riches of the wisdom and knowledge of God! How unsearchable his judgements, and his paths beyond tracing out! 'Who has known the mind of the Lord? Or who has been his counsellor?' 'Who has ever given to God, that God should repay them?'
> ROMANS 11:33–35

We can feel the intensity of his words as he writes, his sense of the majesty of God and the sheer folly of trying to second-guess his plans or advise him what to do. Yet our natural response is to do just that.

Job was mystified by God's dealing with him. He suffered appallingly, even though he was a righteous man, and argued his case before the Almighty. His friends sought rather unhelpfully to counsel him, saying the blame must lie with Job, even though Job knew he had done nothing to deserve such tragedy. Eventually God appeared to Job, appropriately enough in a fearful storm, reminding Job of his sovereign greatness and reducing him to silence. 'Who is this that obscures my plans with words without knowledge?' asks the Lord (Job 38:2). Overwhelmed by the presence of God and the weight of his glory, Job recognises his folly in questioning the ways of God and falls to his knees in repentance. 'Surely I spoke of things I did not understand,' he says, 'things too wonderful for me to know' (Job 42:3). No answer is ever given to Job to explain his suffering. In the end, confronted by the presence of God, he needs none. It is sufficient to know that God is in control.

Mystery lies at the heart of the Christian faith. It is there in the doctrine of the Trinity, in the incarnation and at the cross. We encounter it in our prayer lives and in the healing ministry. We meet it too in the providence of God and the outworking of his plans for our lives. Each of us must bow humbly before the greatness of God:

> 'For my thoughts are not your thoughts, neither are your ways my ways,' declares the Lord. 'As the heavens are higher than the earth, so are my ways higher than your ways and my thoughts than your thoughts.'
> ISAIAH 55:8–9

Adjusting to the idea of mystery is actually a liberating experience. It frees us from our compulsive need to supervise the universe and advise God on what he should do next. Instead we can relax, knowing that his wisdom and love have everything under control. In fact, we end up with a bigger God than we had before. Furthermore, it creates in us an appropriate humility and brings us to a place of calm contentment. The psalmist says:

> My heart is not proud, Lord, my eyes are not haughty; I do not concern myself with great matters or things too wonderful for me. But I have calmed and quieted myself, I am like a weaned child with its mother; like a weaned child I am content.
> PSALM 131:1–2

My own journey in this area continues. I now feel less need to have everything figured out. I often say that I am less certain, but more sure. By this I mean there are many things I no longer profess to understand about God and his ways, but that is alright. My faith may be less tidy than it was before, and there are more loose ends, but at its core my faith is stronger than ever because it is rooted in the goodness and love of God.

# Conversation starters

1  How do you respond to the author's personal story?
2  Has there been anything in your own life that has made you question your faith or your presuppositions? How have you dealt with such issues?
3  Do you recognise in yourself the tendency to want to fathom everything? Why is this unhelpful?
4  Is your God too small? How does mystery fit into your understanding and experience of God?
5  Why do you think the author says, 'Mystery lies at the heart of the Christian faith'? Do you agree?

# Helpful reading

Halcyon Backhouse (ed.), *The Cloud of Unknowing* (Hodder Classics, 2009)
Ron Dunn, *When Heaven is Silent: Trusting God when life hurts* (CLC, 1994)
Tony Horsfall, *Deep Calls to Deep: Spiritual formation in the hard places of life* (BRF, 2015)
Brian D. McLaren, *Naked Spirituality: A life with God in twelve simple words* (Hodder and Stoughton, 2010)
Christopher J.H. Wright, *The God I Don't Understand: Reflections on tough questions of faith* (Zondervan, 2008)

# 29

# God's purpose in suffering

**Who shall separate us from the love of Christ? Shall trouble or hardship or persecution or famine or nakedness or danger or sword?...
No, in all these things we are more than conquerors through him who loved us.**
ROMANS 8:35, 37

As I begin to write this chapter I have received news of a tragic road accident involving two couples in senior leadership roles within an international Christian organisation. Of the four, three died at the scene, and the other one, plus the driver of the vehicle, is in hospital seriously injured. What a tragedy. It is a devastating blow to all who knew them, to their families and friends and to their organisation. It seems at this moment to be unfair, unnecessary and hard to understand.

A friend reminds me, quite rightly, that road traffic accidents are common throughout the world and that as Christians we are not sheltered from such harsh realities. They touch our lives as well as the lives of others. It is part of sharing the human condition. We live in a broken, fallen world, which is not now as God intended it to be (although one day it will be made good again). Bad things happen to good people, and we all feel pain and hurt.

The reality of suffering will touch each of our lives in some way, at some time. It comes in many forms – the scourge of cancer, the pain of a marriage or relationship breakdown, a sudden redundancy, financial problems, children going off the rails. We have to work out in our own minds a theology of suffering, a way of interpreting such ghastly events so we make some kind of sense out of them and can live again, albeit never the same as before. But that is not easy. Here are some simple pointers.

## God weeps with us in our pain

One thing we do know is that God weeps with us in our pain. He does not stand aloof, detached, unfeeling. The incarnation reminds us that he became Immanuel, God with us. He took our flesh and blood, lived our life and suffered as we suffer, and he identifies with us in our pain. Only thus could he become a merciful and faithful high priest, bringing comfort to us in our time of need. He is the man of sorrows, acquainted with grief (Isaiah 53:3). As the Father of mercies and God of all comfort, he is able to comfort us in all our troubles, as the apostle Paul discovered (2 Corinthians 1:3–4). He does this through the work of the Comforter (the Holy Spirit), who brings peace amid the storm, and through the love and presence of other people. Somehow we learn in the midst of our pain not to rely on ourselves but to depend more fully on God, who alone can sustain us.

## Death is not the end

We also remember that death is not the end, that tragedy does not have the final word. For those who trust in Jesus there is the hope of heaven, the conviction that leaving this life is to be ushered into God's presence. The pain of loss and separation is real, but it need not defeat us, since we believe in the reality of heaven. We must grieve, and we must grieve well, but grief need not ultimately overwhelm us, for we have a sure and certain hope that serves as an anchor for our souls. One day we will be reunited (1 Thessalonians 4:13–18; Hebrews 6:19). Knowing this helps us find perspective in our suffering. This life is not all there is. There is a life to come and an eternal glory that will far outweigh the sadness we feel here on earth. For this reason, we choose to fix our eyes not on what is seen but on what is as yet unseen (2 Corinthians 4:16–18).

## The bigger picture

With the passing of time we may well begin to see the bigger picture of what God has been doing through our suffering, whatever form it takes. Scripture tells us that nothing can separate us from the love of God, no hardship or tribulation cut us adrift from our security in him:

> Do you think anyone is going to be able to drive a wedge between us and Christ's love for us? There is no way! Not trouble, not hard times, not hatred, not hunger, not homelessness, not bullying threats, not backstabbing, not even the worst sins listed in Scripture.
>
> ROMANS 8:38 (MSG)

But more than that, there is the assurance that somehow God can bring good out of evil and transform negative events into positive ones. Paul writes, 'And we know that in all things God works for the good of those who love him, who have been called according to his purpose' (Romans 8:28). Joseph discovered this truth in his own life after being rejected by his brothers and sold as a slave into Egypt. God was in fact sending him ahead of his family, so that, having been raised to a high position by God, he was able to save his family when famine hit their land. He declared, 'You intended to harm me, but God intended it for good to accomplish what is now being done, the saving of many lives' (Genesis 50:20; see also 45:4–8).

Such purposes are best seen with hindsight. At the time all seems dark, but later we can often see how good things have come out of bad situations. This is why many people, when facing extreme suffering, give themselves to campaigning to change things so that their loved ones did not die in vain. They want good to come out of it, and so does God. Our loss may improve things for other people. Lessons can be learned, changes made, conditions improved.

## Suffering produces character

Another long-term consequence of suffering is that God uses it to change and transform us. Suffering may indeed be an unwelcome guest in our lives, but it is one of the main ways by which God is able to change us and make us into deeper, better and more mature individuals. Indeed, Scott Shaum, speaking out of his own suffering and experience of helping others through adversity, states this very clearly: 'God has created the human soul so it requires some element of suffering to reach its full depth of maturity.'[49]

God does not punish us with suffering, but he may use suffering to refine us and purify us, just like gold in the refiner's fire (1 Peter 1:6–7). Trials have the effect of bringing to the surface attitudes and motivations that need to be changed so that our faith is stronger and purer, cleansed from self-centredness. Furthermore, hardship and adversity test the genuineness of our faith. Do we believe in God only when things are going well or can we trust him through our difficulties (James 1:12)? In the crucible we find our values are tested. We see the shallowness of much that is earthly and the greater worth of that which is heavenly.

Added to this, such testing produces character within us. We learn to persevere (James 1:2–4; Romans 5:3–4). Often we are made more humble and compassionate and can sympathise more deeply with others. We become better listeners, people who are able to comfort others. Such maturation would not happen without the experience of suffering. It smooths our rough edges and softens our hardness, helping us in the long run to become a little more like Jesus.

At best we have only a partial understanding of why God allows suffering. We have some glimpses into what may be happening, but that is all. We must beware of trite answers and of patronising with glib responses those who suffer. Sometimes there seems to be no clear-cut answer, and we are left with the mystery of God's will. Ultimately we must choose to trust God and to believe in his goodness and wisdom and the outworking of his plan and purpose. His ways are not our ways, and his thoughts are not our thoughts – they are higher than ours, beyond our comprehension (Isaiah 55:8–9).

This God whom we serve is unfathomable to human minds, but he is good, loving and faithful in all that he does. That is why when we trust him through the darkness, we glorify him the most. Our trust brings him immense pleasure because it is the greatest expression of love. Thus, as Brennan Manning says, 'It may mean more to Jesus when we say, "I trust you", than when we say, "I love you."'[50]

## Conversation starters

1   What has been your experience of suffering? How have you dealt with it?
2   This chapter gives some glimpses into what may be happening in our suffering. Which helps you the most, and why?
3   How might God use suffering to bring us to maturity?
4   What can we learn here about how to help another person who is suffering?
5   How do you understand the quotation from Brennan Manning? Why is trust the highest expression of love?

# Helpful reading

Mags Duggan, *God among the Ruins: Trust and transformation in difficult times* (BRF, 2018)

Ron Dunn, *When Heaven is Silent: Trusting God when life hurts* (CLC, 2013)

Timothy Keller, *Walking with God through Pain and Suffering* (Hodder and Stoughton, 2013)

Brennan Manning, *Ruthless Trust: The ragamuffin's path to God* (SPCK, 2002)

Scott E. Shaum, *The Uninvited Companion: God's shaping us in his love through life's adversities* (Cresta Riposos Books, 2017)

# 30

# Understanding providence

**Now I want you to know, brothers and sisters, that what has happened to me has actually served to advance the gospel. As a result, it has become clear throughout the whole palace guard and to everyone else that I am in chains for Christ.**
PHILIPPIANS 1:12–13

Providence is the belief that God is guiding human affairs, both good and bad, to bring about his ultimate good purposes. We may not always understand what he is doing at the time, but eventually we can often see how God has shaped things for our good. Providence is best seen with hindsight and requires the eye of faith – it is a way of interpreting the events of our lives, making sense of the ups and the downs. It can be defined as: 'God our heavenly Father working in and through all things by his wisdom and power for the good of his people and the glory of his name.'[51]

It used to be that in Christian countries most people interpreted their lives through the lens of providence. Nowadays, in an age of self-determination, people are more inclined to believe that we shape our own destiny, or that we are more at the mercy of fate or chance than the purpose of God. Even churches fail to teach about providence, so a whole generation of disciples has grown up without knowing the reassuring benefits of this biblical doctrine.

Paul's imprisonment in Rome may have appeared to be a setback for the spread of the gospel, but he discovered that God had a plan for him even in his confinement. It gave him the opportunity to testify to his guards and other prisoners, and his boldness made his fellow believers more bold in their witness (Philippians 1:12–14). In the providence of God what looked like a negative circumstance was turned to a positive opportunity.

Paul had many such experiences, and he articulates the truth of providence most clearly in Romans 8:28: 'And we know that in all things God works for the good of those who love him, who have been called according to his purpose.' It is worth highlighting several truths contained in these words:

- It is God who brings good out of our circumstances. It is not the circumstances themselves that are good; they may well not be good. It requires the action of God to bring good out of what may be best described as evil.

- No circumstance is outside of God's control – 'all things' means all things.

- While God's providence can be seen in the world in a general way, it is especially noticed in the lives of those who love God and in whom his purpose – to become like Christ – is being worked out (Romans 8:29). Providence is a crucial ingredient, therefore, in our spiritual formation.

- Providence does not mean that God is the author of evil. Not everything that happens to us is caused by God, but everything that happens to us is under his control and in the end will serve his purpose for us. We make a distinction between God's *directive* will (what he causes to happen) and his *permissive* will (what he allows to happen in respecting human freedom). We live in a fallen world, where natural disasters occur and affect us all (Romans 8:22); sinful human beings hurt one another; we make bad choices ourselves; and Satan is responsible for a lot of the world's evil. Yet God remains in control and, despite all the mess and interference with his plans, can still bring good to pass and accomplish his purposes.

Reflecting on this scripture, Alistair Begg says:

This great verse is a promise from God that we are not the hapless victims of life, at the mercy of chance or fate. We are not driven by some blind, impersonal force. On the contrary, we are the objects of God's providential care. We are under his guiding and protecting hand.[52]

The story of Joseph (Genesis 37—50) beautifully illustrates this belief in the providence of God. Sold into slavery by his brothers, Joseph is taken down into Egypt and finds himself serving in the household of Potiphar, a royal official. God was with Joseph and he gained favour before Potiphar, until he was wrongly accused of sexually harassing his master's wife. Thrown into jail, he languished there for two whole years, but again the Lord was with him and he was given a place of responsibility within the prison. Because of his ability to interpret dreams, he was taken to Pharaoh and asked to give the meaning of the ruler's dream. With God's help, Joseph saw that the country would have a time of plenty followed by a time of famine, and he advised Pharaoh how to steward food supplies during the coming years. His plan worked and once more Joseph was raised to prominence, becoming second only to Pharaoh in the whole land. Both his suffering and his success were due to God's ordering of the events of his life. God was with him as much in the prison as in the palace.

When famine came, there was food throughout Egypt because of Joseph's God-given strategy. Back in Israel his family did not fare so well, and Jacob sent his sons down to Egypt to look for help. Amazingly it was Joseph to whom they made their appeal, although they did not recognise him. Once he was sure of their sincerity, he revealed himself to them, recognising that God had ordained the whole set of circumstances in his life so that he would be in a position to help his family at a crucial moment. He said to them:

> I am your brother Joseph, the one you sold into Egypt! And now, do not be distressed and do not be angry with yourselves for selling me here, because it was to save lives that *God sent me ahead of you*… God sent me ahead of you to preserve for you a remnant on earth and to save your lives by a great deliverance.
>
> GENESIS 45:4–5, 7 (my italics)

Joseph was able to come to terms with what had happened to him because he could see how God had orchestrated the events of his life towards a higher purpose.

With this perspective Joseph was able to forgive his brothers. He explains his understanding of their story as an expression of God's providence: 'You intended to harm me, but God intended it for good to accomplish what is now being done, the saving of many lives. So then, don't be afraid. I will provide for you and your children' (Genesis 50:20–21). In the providence of God, evil has been turned to good, and God's purpose has been worked out even through the sinful actions of those involved. This is the amazing beauty of providence, and it is at work in your life and mine.

Eric Liddell, the famous Olympic athlete and missionary to China who died during Japanese internment in 1945, wrote, 'Circumstances may appear to wreck our lives and God's plans, but God is not helpless among the ruins. God's love is still working. He comes in and takes the calamity and uses it victoriously, working out His wonderful plan of love.'[53] These are the assurances we can have when we understand the providence of God and see our lives from God's perspective.

## Conversation starters

1  How do you understand the providence of God?
2  Why do you think it is less popular today than in previous generations?
3  What other examples of providence can you see in scripture?
4  Can you give an example of God's providence in your own life?
5  Why does the teaching about God's providence give us great assurance?

## Helpful reading

Alistair Begg, *The Hand of God: Finding his care in all circumstances* (Moody, 1999)
John Flavel, *The Mystery of Providence* (Banner of Truth Trust, 1991)
John Sanders, *The God Who Risks: A theology of divine providence*, revised edition (IVP, 2007)
Melvin Tinker, *Intended for Good: The providence of God* (IVP, 2012)

# Notes

1   David G. Benner, *Sacred Companions: The gift of spiritual friendship and direction* (IVP, 2002), ch. 2.
2   Benner, *Sacred Companions*, p. 54.
3   The Puritans were members of a religious reform movement known as Puritanism that arose within the Church of England in the late 16th century. They believed the Church of England was too similar to the Roman Catholic Church and should eliminate ceremonies and practices not rooted in the Bible. They were known for their spirituality and godly way of life.
4   Joanne J. Jung, *The Lost Discipline of Conversation: Surprising lessons in spiritual formation drawn from the English Puritans* (Zondervan, 2018), p. 17.
5   Jung, *The Lost Discipline of Conversation*, p. 18.
6   Gordon MacDonald, *Building below the Waterline: Shoring up the foundations of leadership* (Hendrickson, 2011), p. 1.
7   Bill Hull, *The Complete Book of Discipleship: On being and making followers of Christ* (NavPress, 2006), p. 16.
8   Charles W. Colson, *Born Again* (Chosen Books, 2008), p. 10.
9   John Stott, *Focus on Christ* (Collins, 1979), p. 54.
10  Stott, *Focus on Christ*, p. 60.
11  Andrew Murray, *Abide in Christ* (Nisbet and Co, c. 1895), p. 45.
12  Norman P. Grubb, *The Liberating Secret* (Lutterworth Press, 1955).
13  Lloyd John Ogilvie, *You are Loved and Forgiven* (Regal Books, 1977), pp. 72–74.
14  Henri Nouwen, *The Return of the Prodigal Son: A story of homecoming* (Darton, Longman and Todd, 1994), p. 16.
15  David G. Benner, *Surrender to Love: Discovering the heart of Christian spirituality* (IVP, 2003), p. 92.
16  Evangelical Alliance (UK) statement of faith: **eauk.org/about-us/basis-of-faith**.
17  **biblesociety.org.uk/explore-the-bible/the-bible-course**
18  Richard Foster, *Celebration of Discipline: The path to spiritual growth* (Hodder and Stoughton, 1980), p. 115.
19  Frederick Buechner, *Listening to your Life* (HarperSanFrancisco, 1992), p. 186.
20  Helen Coffey, 'Why "admitting" you are a Christian at work is so very hard', *The Daily Telegraph*, 31 March 2014: **telegraph.co.uk/women/womens-life/10733863/Why-admitting-you-are-a-Christian-at-work-is-so-very-hard.html**.

21  Steve Hoke and Bill Taylor, *Global Mission Handbook: A guide for crosscultural service* (IVP, 2009), p. 174.
22  Debbie Hawker and Tim Herbert (eds), *Single Mission: Thriving as a single person in cross-cultural ministry* (Condeo Press, 2013), p. 13.
23  Hawker and Herbert, *Single Mission*, p. 15.
24  Sheridan Voysey, *Resurrection Year: Turning broken dreams into new beginnings* (Thomas Nelson, 2013) deals with the issue of being childless in marriage.
25  Gary Chapman, *The Five Love Languages* (Northfield Publishing, 1992).
26  For example the Thomas Kilmann Conflict Mode Instrument: **kilmanndiagnostics.com**.
27  See **talkingjesus.org/research**.
28  Matthew Knell, 'Just like my Father', *IDEA Magazine* (Evangelical Alliance UK), September/October 2019, p. 3.
29  Roger Steer, *Inside Story: The life of John Stott* (IVP, 2009), p. 161.
30  Tom Christmas, 'A just generation', *IDEA Magazine* (Evangelical Alliance UK), September/October 2019, p. 15. See also **justloveuk.com**
31  Foster, *Celebration of Discipline*, p. 6.
32  Andrew Roberts, *Holy Habits: Introductory guide* (BRF, 2018), p. 7.
33  Pete Greig, *The Vision and the Vow: A call to discipleship* (Kingsway, 2005), p. 149.
34  David G. Benner, *The Gift of Being Yourself: The sacred call to self-discovery*, expanded edition (IVP, 2015), p. 31.
35  Examples of other psychometric tests include Belbin's Team Roles and the Thomas Kilmann Instrument (TKI) for conflict resolution. Many people find the Enneagram helpful from a spiritual perspective.
36  Richard Foster, *Money, Sex and Power: The challenge of the disciplined life* (Hodder and Stoughton, 1985), p. 1.
37  Keith Farmer, quoted in Rick Lewis, *Mentoring Matters* (Monarch, 2009), pp. 234–35.
38  Derek Tidball, *Wisdom from Heaven: The message of the letter of James for today* (Christian Focus, 2003), p. 23.
39  Tony Horsfall and Debbie Hawker, *Resilience in Life and Faith: Finding your strength in God* (BRF, 2019), pp. 8–9.
40  Karen Carr, quoted by Debbie Hawker in Horsfall and Hawker, *Resilience in Life and Faith*, p. 14.
41  Richard Swenson, *Margin: Restoring emotional, physical, financial, and time reserves to overloaded lives* (NavPress, 2004), p. 57.
42  Stephen W. Smith, *Soul Custody: Choosing to care for the one and only you* (David C. Cook, 2010), p. 29.
43  Watchman Nee, *Sit, Walk, Stand* (Victory Press, 1957), p. 13.
44  Marva J. Dawn, *Keeping the Sabbath Wholly: Ceasing, resting, embracing, feasting* (Eerdmans, 1989), p. 4.

45   Brennan Manning, *Abba's Child: The cry of the heart for intimate belonging* (NavPress, 1994), p. 59.

46   Eugene Peterson, *A Long Obedience in the Same Direction: Discipleship in an instant society* (IVP, 1980).

47   Janet O. Hagberg and Robert A. Guelich, *The Critical Journey: Stages in the life of faith* (Sheffield Publishing Company, 2005).

48   Buechner, *Listening to Your Life*, p. 186.

49   Scott Shaum in Frauke C. Schaefer and Charles A. Schaefer (eds), *Trauma and Resilience: A handbook – effectively supporting those who serve God* (self-published, 2012), p. 17.

50   Brennan Manning, *Ruthless Trust: The ragamuffin's path to God* (SPCK, 2002), p. 181.

51   Melvin Tinker, *Intended for Good: The providence of God* (IVP, 2012), p. 20.

52   Alistair Begg, *The Hand of God: Finding his care in all circumstances* (Moody, 1999), p. 9.

53   Eric Liddell, *The Disciplines of the Christian Life* (SPCK, 2009), p. 122.

**BRF** *Enabling all ages to grow in faith*

Anna Chaplaincy
Living Faith
Messy Church
Parenting for Faith

**The Bible Reading Fellowship (BRF)** is a Christian charity that resources individuals and churches. Our vision is to enable people of all ages to grow in faith and understanding of the Bible and to see more people equipped to exercise their gifts in leadership and ministry.

To find out more about our ministries and programmes, visit

**brf.org.uk**